Painting
Wildlife & Birds

WILLOW WOLFE

All American **Crafts**
Publishing, Inc.

Painting Wildlife & Birds

All American Crafts, Inc.
7 Waterloo Road
Stanhope, NJ 07874
www.allamericancrafts.com

Publisher: Jerry Cohen
Chief Executive Officer: Darren Cohen
Art Director: Kelly Alberston
Copy Editing: Mary Ellen Bruno
Editorial Advisor: Linda Heller
Product Development Director: Brett Cohen

Every effort has been made to ensure that the information presented is accurate. Since we have no control over physical conditions, individual skills, or chosen tools and products, the publisher disclaims any liability for injuries, losses, untoward results, or any other damages which may result from the use of the information in this book. Thoroughly read the instructions for all products used to complete the projects in this book, paying particular attention to all cautions and warnings shown for that product to ensure their proper and safe use.

Printed in China
©2009 All American Crafts, Inc
ISBN-13: 978-0-9789513-9-9
ISBN-10: 0-9789513-9-5
Library of Congress Control Number: 2009930408

SPECIAL THANKS TO:

- Howard at Princeton Art and Brush Company;

- Linda Heller at *Paintworks* Magazine;

- Janeen, Bart, Gerry, and the staff at Artists Emporium whose expert framing made the work shine;

- and the many suppliers of surfaces, paints, and brushes who gave so generously.

ACKNOWLEDGMENTS

For their contribution of brushes,
Princeton Art and Brush Company
Suite 123 CN 5256,
Princeton, NJ 08543
www.princetonartandbrush.com

PaintWorks® Magazine
All American Crafts, Inc.
7 Waterloo Road, Stanhope, NJ 07874
www.paintworksmag.com

For FolkArt® *Acrylic Colors*
Plaid Enterprises, Inc.
www.plaidonline.com

For oil paint, Martin F. Weber
www.weberart.com

For palette,
Masterson Art Products, Inc.
www.mastersonart.com
(800) 965-2675

For framing, Artists Emporium, 1610 St. James Street, Winnipeg, MB R3H 0L2 Canada
(800) 665-0322
www.artistsemporium.net

For leafing products,
Mona Lisa Products, Speedball Art Products, www.speedballart.com

For surfaces,
Turn of the Century Wood Products
www.turnofthecentury-in.com

Coyote Woodworks
www.coyotewoodworks.net

The Artists Club, www.artistsclub.com

Western Metal Ware
www.westernmetalware.com

For stencils, Rebecca Baer, Inc.
www.rebeccabaer.com

About the Author

Willow Wolfe

Willow is an accomplished artist with a gift for painting in oil, acrylic, and watercolor, creating dramatic and fluid images that attract audiences around the world. Her whimsical style reflects a strong belief in the wonders and beauty of nature, with vivid representations of animals, birds, and flowers that touch the imagination, and illustrate the extreme inspirations of subtle grace.

Willow's inspiring ability to paint and teach about wildlife have made her a popular and sought-after instructor throughout North America. She is an author of numerous books and articles, and she is featured at international conventions and various major cities for specialized seminars. You can find her signature line of painting kits, design packets, and books online at www.willowwolfe.ca. Currently, Willow resides in Winnipeg, Manitoba, Canada, with her greatest inspiration yet—her beautiful daughter, Nya.

Thank You

To the students, teachers, and suppliers who make my dreams come alive on canvas and in print, and to everyone I've met along the way.

To my parents for helping me put foundations under those castles in the sky.

To my friends who are exceptional!

Special Thanks To:

- Howard and Peter at Princeton Art and Brush Co.
- Brett and Linda and the crew at All American Crafts.
- Janeen, Bart, Gerry, and the staff at Artists Emporium whose expert framing made the work shine.
- The many suppliers of surfaces, paints, and brushes who gave so generously.
- Speedball Art Products for the best in metal leafing supplies and accessories, and the most beautifully pigmented acrylic ink.
- Artograph Inc. and the DesignMaster Projector® for creating easy-to-use tools for transferring designs to any surface of any size!

Dedication

To Baby Nya — you are an incredibly funny little joy. For all the times you threw paint at me on the patio, for every moment spent watching little birdies eat from our feeders, for the 50 permanent marker happy faces on your wall, and for every time I hear you say, "I love you, Mommy!" But mostly for being an understanding, kindhearted best friend to share my life with.

Page 50

Page 68

Page 82

Page 114

Page 58

Page 102

CONTENTS

Introduction 8

Painting Supplies 10

General Information
& Techniques 18

Painting Projects 29

Simply Beautiful Butterfly 30

Exotic Butterfly Bowl 32

Peacock Butterfly Canvas 36

Vanessa 40

Pink Orchids & Butterfly 44

Chickadee & Cherries 50

Baby Ducks 58

Guardian Angels Plaque 62

Ruby-Throated Hummingbird Journal 68

Exotic Duo 74

Blue Jay 82

Baby Bunny & Magnolias 86

Doe in the Forest 94

Chipmunk & Fruit 102

Squirrel & Berries 108

The White Tiger 114

Bengal Tiger—Night Gaze 122

Metric Conversion Chart 127

Index 127

Give Your Paintings the Look of Life

If you love the beauty of nature and wish you could paint the birds, animals, and flowers that you see, then this book is for you. Willow Wolfe has a gift for painting the wonders of the natural world and shares her techniques in a step-by-step format even the beginner can enjoy.

The results of each brushstroke are magical! The results you desire can be found in learning where to place sparkling highlights and deep, rich shadows. Learn and practice techniques for soft downy feathers or sleek and smooth fur, and blending techniques that allow for beautiful variations of color within flower petals and leaves. Each and every brushstroke can create a unique and beautiful effect. There are no mistakes when painting wildlife, as each turn of the brush brings a touch of unique life to your subject.

The 17 projects in this book are painted with oil colors on canvas, wood, or metal surfaces. If you prefer painting with acrylics, there is a complete color conversion chart. Every project is accompanied by step-by-step painting worksheets and close-up photos that show you how to place the colors, blend them, and add the lifelike details that make Willow's designs so vivid.

Willow shows you simple ways to enhance your painted projects with dimensional effects, stenciling, and decoupage. Bring your art off the wall when you paint her designs for bowls, a basket cover, and a one-of-a-kind penholder. An experienced teacher as well as a talented artist, Willow is an inspiring guide for your adventure in painting the natural world.

PAINTING SUPPLIES

Brushes, paints, mediums, and a surface for painting—those are only the basics. This section tells you all about the supplies you will need to paint the projects in this book, as well as how to prepare wood, metal, and canvas surfaces for accepting the paint.

Good tools and materials are a necessity, not a luxury. Artist-quality paints and brushes will always give you more satisfying results for the time and attention you devote to a project.

Brushes

Brushes are the tools you use to create your art, and it is essential to purchase the very best. Quality brushes are an absolute necessity. They need to keep a good chisel edge in order to create fluffy feathers and soft fur. Use the brushes listed in this section for all the painting projects. If a specific brush is not listed for painting a certain area, then use the largest brush that will fit the area you are painting.

Note: Keep brushes used for oil painting separate from brushes used for acrylics. The brushes used in this book can be used for oil, acrylic, or watercolor; however, once you've used a brush in a particular medium, it should stay with that medium.

BRIGHTS AND CHISEL BLENDERS

Most of the projects in this book can be painted with brights. They are essentially the same type of brush as a flat, but they have shorter bristles. The shorter bristles allow for better control when blending and for the creation of smooth feather lines and fur. A good bright has a supple enough bristle to blend softly and yet maintain a sharp enough chisel edge for feather and fur painting techniques. A bright brush may also be referred to as a *chisel blender.* **Sizes Needed: #2, #4, #6, #8, #10**

FLAT SHADER

Flat shaders have longer bristles than brights. Use the larger flat shaders for background blending or for basecoating larger areas. Use the smaller ones for painting and blending tiny areas. **Sizes Needed: #0, #2, #10, #12**

WASH

Wash brushes come in several shapes. The projects in this book use the square wash brush in a ¾" width. It is used for basecoating and laying in large areas of color.
Size Needed: ¾"

LINER AND SHORT LINERS

Liners are small round brushes with long hairs that allow for great brush control. They are delicate, so remember to be gentle with them. They are great for eyes, details, and tiny fur and feather lines. To use the liner, thin the paint with odorless turpenoid to the consistency of ink.
Sizes Needed: 18/0, 10/0

LUNAR BLENDER

The lunar blender has a blend of bristles that are quite stiff. Lunars are used for soft, fluffy fur and feathers, as well as foilage.

GRAINER

The grainer has bristles of uneven lengths, so that it can create multiple fine lines with a single stroke. In addition to fur and downy feathers, the grainer can be used to create striations on florals, butterflies, and birds. This brush may also be referred to as a *filbert comb*.
Sizes Needed: ⅜", ½"

MOP

Mop brushes have a soft, thick, rounded shape. Use a mop as a finishing tool to soften blending and brushstrokes. Do not soften too much; it is easy to overuse mops. During use, wipe the brush on soft, absorbent paper towels, but do not clean with thinner until you are finished painting.
Size Needed: ½"

BRUSH CARE & CLEANING FOR OIL PAINTS

- Before using a brush for the first time, remove the sizing in the bristles with baby oil.
- To clean the paint from a brush during use, wipe it within the folds of a paper towel; do not clean brushes with thinners unless you are finished painting.
- Clean your brushes when you have finished a painting session.

Steps for final cleaning
1. Dry-wipe the brush between the folds of a paper towel to remove excess paint.
2. Dip the brush in odorless turpenoid and gently blot it on a soft paper towel. Repeat several times.
3. Pour baby oil in the palm of your hand and gently pull the brush hairs through the oil. Blot on a soft paper towel. When the oil is dirty, replace it and continue. It may take several minutes to clean the brush thoroughly.

Pictured top to bottom: #10, #8, #6, #4, #2 brights

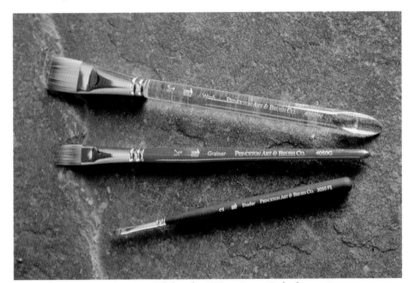

Pictured top to bottom: 3/4" wash brush, 1/2" grainer, #2 shader

Pictured top to bottom: 3/4" filbert grainer, 1/2" grainer, 1/2" oval mop, #10 chisel blender, 3/4" oval mop, 1" oval mop, 1/2" lunar blender, 1" lunar blender

Oil Paints

To create the luminosity of a butterfly's wings or the depth of color on brilliant bird feathers, it is absolutely essential to use good-quality paints. The projects in this book were created with artist-quality oil paints. Oils are easy to work with for any level of painting skill, last forever, and have a wonderful consistency.

NOTE: You may paint these projects in acrylic if you prefer. It is equally important to purchase good-quality, heavy-body acrylics in order to layer and blend the paint.

LOW ODOR THINNER / ODERLESS TURPENOID

This is a solvent used to thin the paint while painting and to clean liner brushes between uses. Low odor thinner has less odor than turpentine. It should always be kept in a small-capped glass jar.

LINSEED OIL

Linseed oil, derived from flax seeds, is the most commonly used medium for oil paints, making the paints more fluid, transparent, and glossy. Use linseed oil for glazing after a painting has completely dried. Remember that although the painting might feel dry to the touch, there are layers underneath that may still be wet, so give it ample time — about 30 days — to dry before glazing.

You can use glazing to enhance or intensify an area. Wet the surface with a small amount of medium. Load the brush in a small amount of the desired color, work into the bristles, and apply to the area. Blend with the brush or mop to soften.

Oil Palette

These oil paint colors are used to paint the designs in this book.
The colors used to paint an individual project are listed with the
project instructions. (If you prefer to use acrylics, see the
Conversion Chart in the "Acrylic Paints" section.)

Alizarin Crimson

Burnt Sienna

Burnt Umber

Cadmium Red Deep

*Cadmium Red Light
(Hue)*

Cadmium Red Medium

Cadmium Yellow Light

*Cadmium Yellow Pale
(Hue)*

Cerulean Blue

Cobalt Blue

Cobalt Turquoise

Dioxazine Purple

French Ultramarine

Ivory Black

Lemon Yellow

Magenta

Payne's Gray

Prussian Blue

Raw Sienna

Raw Umber

Sap Green

Titanium White

Ultramarine Blue

Venetian Red

Yellow Green

Yellow Ochre

Acrylic Paints

The designs in this book can be painted using acrylics, if you prefer. The instructions are written for oil paints, so you will need to refer to the Conversion Chart for the equivalent colors of acrylic paints. Use the size and type of brush given in the instructions. Oils and acrylics require different mediums, and acrylics dry more quickly, but the colors and effects will be equally as attractive. Acrylic paints are always used to basecoat the project surface.

PAINTS

Artists' tube acrylics (and oil paints) are manufactured with true pigments. By using the appropriate mediums, you can mix and blend them as you would mix and blend oil paints. They are available at art supply stores.

Bottled artists' pigment acrylics are creamy and opaque, and have true pigment color names. Mix and blend them with the same mediums that you would use for tube acrylics. You will find these paints in squeeze bottles at art supply and craft stores. They are great for backgrounds.

Premixed acrylic craft paints are available in hundreds of colors. They have the same consistency as artists' pigment acrylics and also come in squeeze bottles. While they may be used for basecoating, they are not suitable for the wildlife and nature painting techniques in this book.

MEDIUMS

Mix liquid or gel mediums with your acrylic paints to achieve specific effects. For the best results, use mediums and paints made by the same manufacturer.

Blending gel medium is used to keep acrylic paint wet and movable. Brush the medium on the surface in the area of the design where you are working. Apply paint immediately, while the medium is wet.

Floating medium is used to thin acrylic paints. Fill your brush with floating medium, pick up paint, and blend by stroking the brush on a clear space on your palette.

Glazing medium is used to dilute acrylic paint so the mixture can be used for transparent effects. Mix glazing medium with paint on the palette or in a small container until you achieve the transparent color you want. This medium can be used as a substitute for floating medium.

Water can be used to thin paint for line work and washes.

Conversion Chart

Oil Color		Acrylic Color
Alizarin Crimson	=	Crimson Alizarin
Burnt Sienna	=	Burnt Sienna
Burnt Umber	=	Burnt Umber
Cadmium Red Deep	=	Cadmium Red Medium & Alizarin Crimson
Cadmium Red Light (Hue)	=	Napthol Crimson
Cadmium Red Medium	=	Cadmium Red Medium
Cadmium Yellow Light	=	Yellow Light
Cadmium Yellow Pale (Hue)	=	Yellow Light
Cerulean Blue	=	Aqua + Brilliant Ultramarine
Cobalt Blue	=	Cobalt Blue
Cobalt Turquoise	=	Aqua
Dioxazine Purple	=	Dioxazine Purple
French Ultramarine	=	Brilliant Ultramarine
Ivory Black	=	Mars Black or Ivory Black
Lemon Yellow	=	Yellow Light
Magenta	=	Magenta
Payne's Gray	=	Payne's Gray
Prussian Blue	=	Prussian Blue
Raw Sienna	=	Raw Sienna
Raw Umber	=	Raw Umber
Sap Green	=	Sap Green
Titanium White	=	Titanium White
Ultramarine Blue	=	Brilliant Ultramarine
Venetian Red	=	Cad. Red Med. + Burnt Sienna
Yellow Green	=	Sap Green + Yellow Light
Yellow Ochre	=	Yellow Ochre

Additional Supplies for Painting with Acrylics

You will need the same supplies for preparing surfaces and transferring designs, whether you are painting with oils or acrylics. When painting with acrylics, you will need a few additional items.

Water basin or other container filled with water for rinsing brushes.

Water base brush-on or spray varnish for finishing.

BRUSHES

Use the same types and sizes of brushes for painting with acrylics as you would use for painting with oils. However, keep the brushes you use for acrylics separate from the brushes you use with oils. Once you have used a brush in a particular medium, it should stay with that medium. Acrylics dry quickly, so rinse your brush immediately after using and clean your brushes thoroughly when you finish painting. A brush will be ruined if acrylic paint dries in the bristles.

BRUSH CARE

1. Rinse brushes between colors in a water basin or other container filled with water.
2. Remove all paint from your brushes with a good brush cleaner when you have finished your painting session.
3. Wipe your brushes on 100% cotton rags or soft, absorbent paper towels.

Cleaning Brushes

1. Gently swish the brush through water in a flip-flop motion to rinse out all the paint. Do not scrub the brush on the bottom of the container; that can damage the bristles.
2. Put some brush cleaner in a small dish. Work the cleaner through the hairs of the brush, and blot on a rag or paper towel. Continue until there is no trace of color on the rag.
3. Gently shape the brush hairs with your fingers. Store the brush so the shape will not be distorted. Rinse the brush in clear water before you use it for your next painting session.

PALETTE

You can use a dry palette or wax-coated paper palette for acrylics, but keep in mind that acrylics dry quickly. Increase the time available for working and blending the colors by keeping the paint moist on a "stay-wet" palette. You can find this type of palette where art supplies are sold.

Using a Wet Palette

There are three parts to a wet palette: a plastic tray, a wet sponge, and special palette paper.

1. Soak the palette paper in water for 12 to 24 hours.
2. Saturate the sponge in water. Do not wring it out, but place the wet sponge in the tray.
3. Place the wet paper on top of the wet sponge.
4. Wipe excess water from the paper with a soft, absorbent rag.
5. Squeeze paint onto the surface of the paper.

To increase the open time for moving and blending acrylics, work in a cool room, and do not allow air to blow on the surface you are painting. Heat and moving air will dry the paint quickly.

FINISHES

Use a water base varnish to finish projects that have been painted with acrylics.

1. Apply brush-on varnish with a synthetic large and soft brush.
2. Apply multiple light coats of a spray finish that is recommended for use with acrylic paints (check the label).

Additional Supplies

In addition to paints and brushes, you will need these supplies to complete
the projects. They are not listed with the individual project instructions,
so you will need to gather them before you begin each painting session.

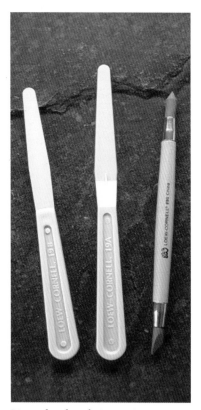

*Pictured:
DesignMaster
Projector®*

Pictured: palette knives, paint eraser

Pictured: transfer paper, stylus

TOOLS

High-density foam roller (4") to apply eggshell finish basecoats

Paint eraser to remove excess paint while painting

Palette knife to mix colors and move paint

Pen or pencil to trace patterns

Ruler to measure and to draw straight lines

Stylus to transfer designs and to draw through wet paint

OTHER NECESSITIES

Baby oil to clean brushes

Brown paper bag (plain) to use as fine sandpaper

Fine-grit sandpaper to smooth surfaces before painting

Lint-free, soft cloth to remove dust particles from the surface after sanding or before varnishing

Masking tape to mask areas where you don't want paint

Palette to lay out paints and mix colors

Small glass jar with lid to keep mediums in while painting

Soft, absorbent paper towels to wipe the brush between uses and for general clean-up

Tracing paper to trace patterns from the book and to use as a palette

White and gray transfer paper to transfer designs

OTHER SUPPLIES

Some projects use these supplies. They will be listed with the instructions for individual projects.

Acrylic ink (acrylic based, water resistant) to stain backgrounds

Gold leaf pen to gild edges and embellishments

Power Wash for removing adhesives

Gold leaf products, including size (adhesive), Adhesive Pen, shellac (sealer), and gold leaf and variegated gold leaf sheets, to add gold leaf to surfaces

Modeling or texture paste to add dimensional elements to surfaces

DesignMaster Projector® for use as an image projector in place of graphite or to enlarge and reduce projects

Surfaces

WOOD

Wooden items in all shapes and sizes make wonderful surfaces for painting. Sand and seal wood surfaces before basecoating.

Preparation

1. Sand, following the direction of the wood grain. Wipe with a slightly damp cloth or a tack cloth to remove all traces of sanding dust.
2. Apply wood sealer. Follow the manufacturer's instructions for application and drying time. Let dry thoroughly.
3. Sand again, or rub the surface with a piece of brown paper bag, which acts as a very fine sandpaper. Wipe with a slightly damp cloth to remove all traces of sanding dust.
4. Basecoat, using a foam roller with acrylic-based paint. Let dry.
5. Rub the surface with a piece of brown paper bag to smooth the basecoat.
6. Apply additional layers of paint until you achieve solid, opaque coverage. Let dry, and rub with a piece of brown paper bag after each coat.
7. Apply the background finish specified in the project instructions.

MASONITE OR HARDBOARD

Lightweight, inflexible, and durable, Masonite or hardboard panels are ready to basecoat. There is no need to sand or seal.

Preparation

1. Basecoat with an acrylic-based paint. Let dry.
2. Rub the surface with a piece of brown paper bag to smooth the basecoat.

3. Apply additional layers of paint until you achieve solid, opaque coverage. Let dry, and rub with a piece of brown paper bag after each coat.
4. Apply the background finish specified in the project instructions.

CANVAS

Tightly woven, springy canvas is a traditional surface for oil paintings. You can buy pre-stretched canvases or canvas paper. Canvas paper is prepared like canvas, but it is smoother and requires less sanding.

Preparation

1. Sand the canvas to smooth it. Wipe with a slightly damp cloth to remove all traces of sanding dust.
2. Basecoat with an acrylic-based paint. Apply as many layers as needed to achieve solid, opaque coverage. Let dry after each layer.
3. Apply the background finish specified in the project instructions.

METAL

Metal surfaces are great for painting, but first you must remove all traces of grease and oil, and roughen the surface so it will hold the paint.

Preparation

1. Clean metal surfaces with vinegar and water. Let dry.
2. Wash with soap and water, rinse well, and let dry.
3. Sand to roughen the metal surface. Wipe with a slightly damp cloth to remove all traces of sanding dust.
4. Spray with a metal primer, preferably gray. Let dry.
5. Basecoat as directed in the project instructions.

GENERAL
INFORMATION
&
TECHNIQUES

From background textures to gold leafing, from brush techniques to tips on painting fur and feathers, you will find easy-to-follow instructions and explanations in this section.

Before you begin to paint the project you have chosen, read the instructions for creating the background, dimensional effects, and embellishments used in the project. Be sure to read the general procedures in "Painting Birds," "Painting Animals," and "Painting Butterflies." Diagrams in those sections will give you the names of specific body parts of birds and insects; you will need to know the terminology in order to follow project instructions. If you plan to paint the projects with acrylics, you will find acrylic painting tips in the sections on painting birds, animals, and butterflies.

Eggshell Finish Background

1. **To create a single color eggshell finish:** Drizzle the acrylic basecoat color directly onto the surface. Use a 4" high-density foam roller to smooth the paint evenly over the surface. Apply several layers of the basecoat color, specified in the project instructions, until you achieve solid, opaque coverage. Let dry, and sand after each coat.

2. **To create a multicolored eggshell finish:** Apply a layer of basecoat color. While the paint is wet, drizzle the other specified colors onto the surface.

3. Using the 4" foam roller, roll in various directions to blend the colors.

Slip-Slap Background

This technique may be used to apply the original acrylic basecoat to the surface, or to apply oil paints for the background of the design.

1. Apply several layers of the acrylic basecoat color specified in the project instructions until you achieve solid, opaque coverage.

2. Apply a fresh layer of the basecoat color, either oil or acrylic. While the paint is wet, use a 1" or ¾" wash brush to pick up the specified colors and slip-slap them into the base color in a crosshatching motion. Before picking up each new color, wipe the brush on a paper towel.

3. Work the various colors into the background, softening and blending the colors. Do not overblend. Allow some brushstrokes to show.

Parchment Background

1. Basecoat with a Warm White acrylic mix (Titanium White acrylic + a touch of Raw Sienna acrylic). Let dry.
2. Use modeling paste or texture paste in a hit-and-miss manner to create texture. Spread the thick paste over the surface with the flat of a palette knife, allowing random areas to show through. Let dry.

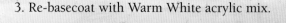

3. Re-basecoat with Warm White acrylic mix.

4. Create a mixture of Burnt Sienna + a touch of Super Black acrylic ink. To this mixture, add water (1:1). Dip a soft, lint-free cloth into the mixture and rub over the surface quickly. If you find it too dark, rub away some of the staining with a clean cloth and clean water.

Metal Leafing

Metal leafing has been used to embellish the surfaces and add a touch of luxury. Objects have been embellished with metal leafing since ancient times, but modern materials and adhesives have greatly simplified the process. Use the products recommended by the manufacturer of the metal leaf sheets and follow the instructions on the label. Metal leaf sheets are extremely thin and light; work in a room with no drafts.

Gather these supplies:
Brushes for applying the basecoat, size, and sealer
Basecoat of choice • Gold leaf size (adhesive)
Metal leaf sheets • Shellac (sealer)
Soft brush for smoothing the gold leaf
Soft, lint-free cloth • Power Wash for cleaning

Here's How:
1. Apply a uniform coat of the basecoat product to the area that will be gold leafed. Wash the brush immediately with soap and water. Allow the basecoat to dry for at least one hour.
2. Apply a thin, even coat of the size (adhesive), making sure there are no puddles. Wash the brush immediately.
3. Allow the size to dry for approximately one hour. It will change from milky white to completely clear, becoming slightly tacky. The gold leaf will not adhere until the size has become clear.
4. With clean, dry hands, pick up a sheet of gold leaf and apply it to the clear size. A razor blade may be helpful to separate the thin sheets. Apply sheets of gold leaf until the area is covered; some overlapping is all right.
5. Remove excess gold leaf by stroking gently with a soft, dry brush. Textural interest is increased when the basecoat shows through small cracks or spots. Large, undesirable spots may be patched by repeating the steps.
6. Apply shellac or sealer, and let dry for the time recommended. Clean the brush with Power Wash.

Acid-free, archival-quality gold leafing adhesive pens are available in several metallic finishes, including gold, silver, and copper. They have chiseled tips that can produce thick or thin lines on wood, fabric, metal, and other surfaces.

Stenciling

Stenciling has been used as an extra design element on some of the projects. Many precut stencils are available, or you could cut a stencil to your own design. Several of the projects in this book include raised patterns created with stencils and modeling paste.

You may also use stencils with paint. Apply the paint sparingly, pouncing with a small sponge applicator or a stencil brush.

How to Stencil:
1. Position the stencil and hold it in place.
2. Apply the acrylic with a brush.
3. Before the acrylic dries completely, remove the stencil by lifting it straight up.

Textured Stenciling

Use texture paste or modeling paste with stencils to create raised designs on your surface. Depending on the look you want, you can wipe the palette knife on a paper towel and smooth the raised design or you can leave it rough.

Here's How:

1. Basecoat the surface. Allow it to dry completely. This example was basecoated with black acrylic paint.
2. Position the stencil and hold it in place. Using a small palette knife, apply paste over the stencil. Remove the stencil before the texture has dried by lifting it straight up. Let the texture dry for several hours. Wash the stencil immediately with soap and water.
3. Paint or work on the stenciled texture as though it were a part of the existing surface. In this example, paints in several greens were applied in a slip-slap method and allowed to dry.
4. To achieve this effect, replace the stencil. Apply metal leaf size with a small round brush and apply leaf, following instructions in "Metal Leafing."

Decoupage

Combining decoupage with paint will allow for a very creative project. Decoupage medium is available in art supply and craft stores. It is used to adhere the paper to the surface as well as to seal and coat the paper. Many beautiful papers are available at art and craft stores.

Here's How:

1. Be sure the surface is dry. Position the paper where desired and mark the placement with a chalk pencil.
2. Place the paper facedown on clean scrap paper and apply decoupage medium to the back.
3. Immediately place the paper in position on the surface. Smooth with your fingers to remove air bubbles and ensure firm contact with the surface. Let dry.
4. Brush decoupage medium over the entire surface of the paper to seal. Apply as many coats as desired, drying after each coat.

Transferring the Design

Use gray transfer paper to transfer designs to light backgrounds and white transfer paper to transfer designs to dark backgrounds.

Here's How:

1. Trace the pattern from the book on tracing paper, using a fine-point permanent marker or a pencil.
2. Position the traced pattern on the surface, and tape it in place with low-tack masking or painter's tape.
3. Slide the transfer paper under the tracing. Be sure the transfer side is down.
4. Go over the pattern lines with a stylus. Use only enough pressure to transfer the pattern, but not so much as to impress lines in the surface.

Finishing

A clear satin spray varnish protects your finished painting from dust and fingerprints, and is quick and easy to apply. Work outdoors or in a well-ventilated area, wear a mask, and follow the manufacturer's safety instructions.

Here's How:

1. Let the painting dry for at least ten days.
2. Clean any unwanted transfer lines from the surface.
3. Hold the can at least 12" from the surface and spray a very light, even coat.
4. Wait until the surface is dry to the touch and spray again. Apply five to ten light coats.

Painting Terms

Basecoating: Painting a solid, opaque layer of paint on the project surface before beginning to paint the design. Several coats may be needed; let each coat dry before applying the next. The surfaces in this book are basecoated with acrylic paints; the designs are painted with oil paints. "Basecoating" can also be used to refer to painting the basic color of a part of the design with oil paint. For example: "Basecoat the beak with Ivory Black." Shading and highlighting values will be blended into the basic color.

Brush loading: Filling a brush with color. To load a bright brush, pull a thin strip of paint from the paint puddle on your palette. Stroke both sides of the brush through the paint, then stroke on the palette to ensure the paint is smooth and has no lumps.

Brush mixing: Picking up first one color, then another color with the brush, allowing the paint to mix in the brush.

Dry-wipe: A technique used to clean the brush without solvent or water. Place the brush between the folds of a paper towel or a soft cloth. Press down and gently pull the brush through the paper towel to remove paint from the bristles.

Floating: This technique is used only when painting with acrylics. Load the brush in floating medium (or water) and blot on a paper towel. Load one corner of the brush in paint. To blend, stroke the brush on a clear area of the palette until you see a smooth gradation from color on one side of the brush to clear medium on the other side.

Glazing: Applying transparent layers of thinned paint to an area to strengthen highlights or shadows, or to add slight tints of color. Be sure the area is completely dry. Apply a thin layer of linseed oil to the surface. Using the same brush, pick up a small amount of the suggested color from your palette and work it into the bristles. Apply to the moistened area, wipe the brush, and blend the color into the area. If desired, mop to soften. Glazing can also be done with acrylics. Use blending gel instead of linseed oil.

Overlay or Overstroke: To lay one layer of fur over another. This term applies when you are adding highlights or shadows or when you are overlapping different colors or values of fur. It is very important to stack the layers of brushstrokes, allowing each preceding layer to show through to create depth and dimension.

Blending Techniques

To create natural effects in your painting, you will frequently need to merge different values and remove a sharp division line where they meet. Blending is usually performed with a chisel blender or bright.

PAT-BLENDING

Blend colors by placing the brush on both colors and gently patting with a "touch-pull" motion where they meet. Use a very light touch and very little paint. Wipe the brush frequently on soft paper towels to remove excess paint.

KEY TIPS FOR BLENDING

- Apply a sparse amount of paint. An excess of paint will become sloppy and move around too much, causing the colors to become muddy.
- Blend where two values meet. Use a very light touch. Wipe the brush frequently or too much of one value will be pulled into the other.
- Soften. When the initial blending is complete, you may want to "whisper" over the blended colors with a mop brush to further soften the brushstrokes and merge the colors.

Marks made by pat-blending with a bright brush.

1. Apply the values.

2. Blend where the values meet.

3. Soften with a mop brush.

CHISEL-BLENDING

Blend values using the chisel edge of the brush. Use this technique to create choppy textures on birds, streaky textures on butterflies, and fur on animals. Follow the growth direction of the subject you are painting, and frequently wipe the brush on soft paper towels to remove excess paint. You can control the color by pulling one value into another, or blend by setting the brush between two colors and wiggling it.

Marks made by chisel-blending with a bright brush.

1. Apply the values.

2. Blend where the values meet by pulling them into each other with the chisel edge of a bright brush.

3. Wipe the brush frequently as you continue to soften the transition of values. Soften further with a mop brush if desired.

STIPPLE-BLENDING

Merge values by tapping with the tip of a liner or round brush.

Marks made by stipple-blending with a liner.

1. Apply the base value.

2. Apply the second value by tapping with the liner (stippling).

3. Wipe the liner frequently and continue to stipple.

4. Add the highlight value and tap to soften. *Note: Each layer of highlight should cover a smaller area than the last.*

Using a Grainer

LOADING THE GRAINER

1. Dip the brush in medium (thinner for oils; water for acrylics).
2. Load the brush in the color.
3. Press the brush firmly onto the palette. Hold it straight up and down and spread the bristles with pressure. Wiggle slightly from side to side.
4. Touch the tips of the brush to a paper towel to remove excess medium.

PAINTING TIPS

1. Use a very light touch. Use some pressure at the beginning of the stroke, then gradually lift the brush as you stroke.
2. Continue to stroke, allowing the brush to run out of paint. A dry brush can be used to stroke over an area for softening.
3. Reload the brush as necessary.

PAINTING ANIMAL FUR

1. Thin the color with low odor thinner until the consistency is creamy (almost wash consistency).
2. Load the grainer on both sides. Press the brush onto the palette and wiggle slightly from side to side to separate the bristles.
3. Gently blot the grainer on a paper towel. Apply light or dark strokes to the desired fur section. Wipe the brush often.
4. Occasionally turn the brush from side to side to vary the strokes and achieve thinner and thicker fur.

1. Apply the first coat with blue + white.

2. Pull blue from the centerline, lifting the brush to leave lighter strokes of paint. Pull blue from the outer edge of the feather toward the centerline, lifting the brush to leave lighter strokes of paint. You should be left with a highlight in the center of each side of the feather.

3. Use the liner to add a white centerline. Add a few fine detail feathers and a shaft line with blue + white. Accent the feather with a liner and thinned crimson + white.

Painting a Bird

OIL PAINTING TIPS

Wings and Tail (Primaries and Coverts):

The long, stiff, major flight feathers are called primaries. Their bases are overlapped by the shorter, softer covert feathers.

1. Basecoat a feather using the chisel edge of the brush to create smooth edges.
2. As you cover transferred pattern lines, draw the feather separation lines back in with the stylus through the wet paint. This will show you where to place the shading and highlighting.
3. To apply feather lines, load the brush with the suggested color. Using the chisel edge and starting at the end of the feather, set the brush down, then pull up into the base of the feather. Starting at the end of the feather allows the brush to pick up the darker basecoat colors of the feather, creating shading and highlighting in one step. If you end up with a chubby feather line, pick up the base color and touch up the feather line from the inside edge.
4. If you want to add extra shading, apply the paint with the chisel edge of the brush where one feather overlaps another. Wipe the brush and drag the shading from the center area of the feather toward the outer edges.

Fluffy Feathers (Down):

1. Basecoat with a bright brush. Use a choppy motion and follow the growth direction of the feathers.
2. Wipe the brush. Block in the different values, placing the shading and highlight colors, following the growth direction.
3. Wipe the brush. Use the chisel edge to blend the color with short, choppy, repetitive strokes.

Glazing (Optional):

Glaze to strengthen highlights or shadows, or to add slight tints of color. Let the painting dry completely, allowing it to cure for several weeks.

1. Brush linseed oil on the area to be glazed.
2. Apply the color.
3. Wipe the brush.
4. Using the chisel edge of the brush, chop or tap the color into the linseed oil to blend and create texture.

Details:

To add extra highlights, use a liner to pull out tiny feathers. If they are too bright, wipe the brush, then gently blend the lines into the base value.

ACRYLIC PAINTING TIPS

The area you are working on should be small enough so that it can be completed before the blending gel dries.

1. Basecoat the various design elements.
2. Apply blending gel medium in a small area. Apply the basecoat color again. Wipe the brush and apply the dark and light values.
3. Use the chisel edge of the brush to blend the values. Follow the growth direction of the feathers and wipe the brush frequently.
4. Float shading under feathers. To begin the stroke, place the dark side of the brush on the area that will have the deepest shade value.
5. Float the highlight color on the top of each feather.
6. Let dry. Glaze to strengthen the dark and light values.
7. Add little feather lines and details with a liner and thinned paint.

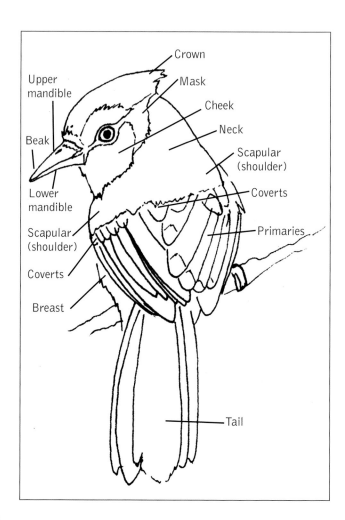

Painting Animals

- Most importantly, follow the growth direction of the fur.
- Paint the eyes, ears, and nose first.
- The fur near the eye and nose is shorter. The fur on the body and tail is longer.
- Remember that each section of fur will overlap the previously painted sections of fur.

OIL PAINTING TIPS

Fur Technique:

1. Begin with the fur near the back of the animal, which is longer and will require longer brushstrokes. Use the chisel edge of a bright brush or the lunar blender to block in the layers of fur. Shorten the brushstrokes as you work toward the eyes and snout.
2. Each new section of fur overlaps the last section of fur. Use the chisel edge of the brush to pull the new color onto the previously painted area. Wipe the brush often so the colors don't become muddy.
3. Use the grainer to overlay the various layers of fur with multiple strokes of highlights and shadows, working the colors into the base value. (*See "Using a Grainer" on page 25.*)
4. Highlight each fur area with overlapping strokes of progressively lighter values. Remember that as you overlap the layers of highlight strokes, the highlighted areas should get smaller and smaller; you are stacking the highlights.
5. When the fur is completed, add detail with the liner. Slightly thin the paint and pull thin lines overlapping each area.

ACRYLIC PAINTING TIPS

1. Basecoat the fur areas, let dry, and re-transfer the details.
2. Paint the eyes, ears, and nose.
3. Use the grainer to apply the initial fur layers. Thin acrylics with water instead of solvent thinner, but follow the same procedure for loading and stroking as for painting with oils.
4. Begin to highlight each fur area with overlapping strokes of progressively lighter values. Remember that as you overlap the layers of highlight strokes, the highlighted areas should get smaller and smaller; you are stacking the highlights.
5. When the fur is completed, add detail with the liner. Slightly thin the paint and pull thin lines, overlapping each area.

Painting Butterflies

OIL PAINTING TIPS

1. Basecoat each area with the color indicated in the instructions, using a small brush. Cover the area solidly, but ensure there are no globs of paint.
2. As you cover transferred pattern lines, draw the segment lines back in with the stylus through the wet paint. This will show you where to paint the wing segment lines and where to place the shading and highlighting.
3. Use the liner to stipple or tap dots of color for the highlights and shading. Wipe the liner and stipple-blend where the new color meets with the basecoat color. Allow the brush to travel in and out of the two areas, softly connecting the colors.
4. To highlight some of the streakier areas, use the chisel edge of the brush to apply the lighter value; wipe the brush and streak through again to soften.
5. To refine the wing, paint the segment lines with the liner and thinned paint, wiping and reloading frequently so as not to muddy the colors.
6. Paint the antennae with the liner and thinned paint. Begin the stroke at the head and lift the pressure as you pull the stroke out in a slight arc.
7. Detail with the liner.

ACRYLIC PAINTING TIPS

The area you are working on should be small enough so that it can be completed before the blending gel dries.

1. Basecoat the various design elements.
2. Apply blending gel medium in a small area. Apply the basecoat color again. Wipe the brush and apply the dark and light values. Blend to soften. Let dry.
3. Float shading and highlights. Let dry.
4. Apply a layer of blending gel. Tap in stronger highlights and shading with the liner. Stipple-blend to merge values and increase texture.

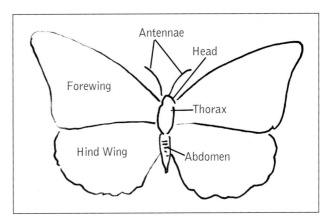

Painting Leaves

TIP: Accent leaves with touches of color from other elements of the painting, or give some dramatic flair to individual leaf tips.

Pat-Blended Leaf

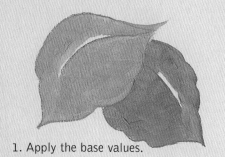

1. Apply the base values.

2. Apply highlights and shading.

3. Pat-blend.

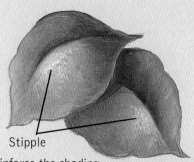

Stipple

4. Reinforce the shading and highlights.

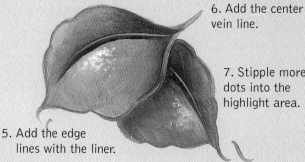

5. Add the edge lines with the liner.

6. Add the center vein line.

7. Stipple more dots into the highlight area.

Chisel-Blended Leaf

1. Apply the dark value.

2. Apply the medium value.

3. Blend with the chisel edge of the brush.

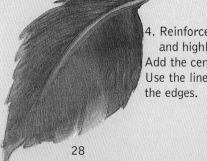

4. Reinforce shading and highlights.
Add the center vein line.
Use the liner to accent the edges.

PAINTING PROJECTS

Here are the complete instructions for 17 lifelike paintings of birds, butterflies, animals, fruits, flowers, and foliage. You will find projects appropriate for many purposes, such as sweet baby ducklings for a child's room, elegant floral designs that make lovely gifts, passionate orchids to please a dramatic personality, and the gaze of a rare tiger to invoke a sense of mystery.

Prepare the surface and gather your brushes, paints, and other supplies before you begin. The project surfaces are basecoated with quick-drying acrylics, but the subjects and backgrounds are painted with oils. Refer to the full-color Painting Worksheets and project photos as you paint.

Keep the list of brushes on hand as listed in the "Painting Supplies" chapter. If a brush size is not listed, use the brush size that best fits the area you are painting.

Most importantly, enjoy the deep satisfaction that comes from creating a work of art that celebrates the beauty of the natural world.

Simply Beautiful Butterfly

This framed and matted painting on canvas paper is subtle yet powerful. Imagine this: A delicate butterfly flutters into a shaft of light. Now paint it! The "light" comes from the placement of subtly blended background colors. The stenciled scrollwork gives an airy, dream-like quality to this little painting.

SUPPLIES

Painting Surface

Canvas paper, 8" x 10"

Oil Palette

Burnt Sienna

Burnt Umber

Cadmium Red Medium

Raw Sienna

Titanium White

Brushes

Bright – #2, #4

Liner – 18/0

Wash – ¾"

Acrylic Background Colors

Raw Sienna

Titanium White

Other Supplies

Stencil – Scrollwork Design

Modeling Paste

Small Coffee Cup, to use as a
    template for the center circle

PREPARATION

Prepare the Surface:

Prepare the canvas, following the instructions in the "Surfaces" section.

Basecoat the Surface:

1. Basecoat the surface with the ¾" wash brush and Titanium White acrylic. Let dry.
2. While the paint is wet, use the wash brush to slip-slap Raw Sienna acrylic into the white. Concentrate the Raw Sienna in the upper right and lower left corners, leaving a diagonal of white "light" as shown in the project photo. Continue in a crosshatching motion until softened and blended. Let dry.

Stencil the Texture:

Refer to the photo for placement. Leave an unstenciled area where the butterfly will be painted.

1. Place the stencil on the surface and hold it down. Place a cup on top of the stencil to allow for a circular area where the butterfly will painted
2. Use a palette knife to spread modeling paste over the stencil; work carefully around the cup. Lift the cup and gently lift the stencil from the surface. Let dry.
3. Repeat the stenciled texture, as needed, to fill the canvas around the butterfly. Let dry.

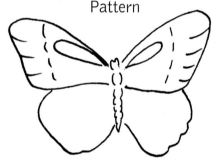

Pattern

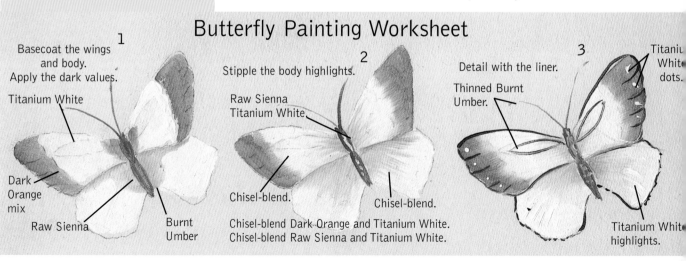

Butterfly Painting Worksheet

1
Basecoat the wings and body.
Apply the dark values.
Titanium White
Dark Orange mix
Raw Sienna
Burnt Umber

2
Stipple the body highlights.
Raw Sienna
Titanium White
Chisel-blend.
Chisel-blend.
Chisel-blend Dark Orange and Titanium White.
Chisel-blend Raw Sienna and Titanium White.

3
Detail with the liner.
Titanium White dots.
Thinned Burnt Umber.
Titanium White highlights.

Prepare to Paint the Design:

1. Trace and transfer the butterfly pattern.
2. Premix the following oil color with a palette knife:
   • Dark Orange: equal parts Cadmium Red Medium + Burnt Sienna

PAINT THE BUTTERFLY

See the Butterfly Painting Worksheet.

1. Basecoat the light sections of the wings with the #4 bright brush and Titanium White.
2. Wipe the brush. Apply Raw Sienna near the body and under the upper wings. Wipe the brush and chisel-blend into the white areas.
3. Basecoat the orange sections with the Dark Orange mix. Wipe the brush and gently connect the values by wiggling the brush softly on the chisel edge.
4. Basecoat the body with the liner and Burnt Umber. While wet, stipple Raw Sienna in the center and stipple-blend to soften.
5. Use the liner and thinned Burnt Umber to add the antennae and details, and line the outer edges of the wings.
6. Use the liner to add Titanium White dots to the upper wings and highlight strokes to the lower wings.

FINISHING

1. Let the painting dry for at least ten days.
2. Apply five to ten coats of spray varnish, drying to the touch after each coat.

31

Exotic Butterfly Bowl

SUPPLIES

Painting Surface
Metal bowl, 10" diameter

Oil Palette
Cadmium Yellow Light
Cobalt Turquoise
Ivory Black
Magenta
Prussian Blue
Sap Green
Titanium White

Brushes
Bright – #2, #4, #6
Liner – 18/0
Wash – ¾"

Acrylic Background Colors
Ivory Black
Sap Green
Yellow Light

Other Supplies
Leaf Stencil, precut Willow Wolfe "Bromeliads" (or cut your own with the pattern provided)
Modeling or Texture Paste
Small Plate or Saucer, to use as a template for the center circle
Gold Leafing Pen or Adhesive Pen
Gold Leaf, Variegated Green or Blue
Gold Leafing Basecoat, Size (Adhesive), and Shellac (Sealer)

The jewel tones of the butterfly and the glimmer of gold leafing transform this metal bowl into a rare treasure. It is a feast for the eyes only; it is not suitable for serving food.

PREPARATION

Prepare the Surface:
Prepare and prime the metal bowl, following the instructions in the "Surfaces" section of the "Supplies" chapter.

Stencil the Texture:
1. Position the leaf stencil and hold it in place.
2. Use a palette knife to spread modeling paste over the stencil. Gently lift the stencil from the surface. Let dry.

Basecoat the Surface:
1. Basecoat the bowl and raised leaf design with the wash brush and Sap Green acrylic. Let dry.
2. Apply a second coat of Sap Green acrylic.
3. While the second coat is wet, pick up a touch of Ivory Black acrylic and slip-slap it into the green.
4. Wipe the brush. Pick up Yellow Light acrylic and slip-slap it into the green and black.
5. Continue working the colors together in a crosshatching motion to achieve a mottled dark green background. Do not overwork. Let dry.

Apply the Gold Leaf:
Refer to the "Metal Leafing" instructions in the "General Information & Techniques" section.
1. Apply the variegated gold leaf to the raised design, following the manufacturer's instructions.
2. Shellac (seal) only the gold leafing. Let dry.

Prepare to Paint the Design:
1. Trace and transfer the butterfly pattern.
2. Premix the following oil color with a palette knife:
   • Pink: equal parts Magenta + Titanium White

Continued on page 34

Continued from page 32

PAINT THE BUTTERFLY

See the Exotic Butterfly Painting Worksheet.

Basecoat the Wings:

1. Basecoat the green areas with the #4 bright brush and Sap Green.
2. Basecoat the pink areas with the Pink mix.

Forewings:

1. Use the #4 bright brush to apply a Cadmium Yellow Light highlight with pressure onto the upper wings. Use the chisel edge of the brush to streak through the highlight toward the outer edges of the wings.
2. Use the liner and thinned Cadmium Yellow Light to add touches of stippled highlight on the outer wings and near the body.
3. Accent the lower edges of the upper wings with the Pink mix. Wipe the brush and chisel-blend.
4. Use the liner to highlight the pink accent areas with stippled dots of Titanium White.

Hind Wings:

1. Apply the shadow under the upper wings with Prussian Blue. Wipe the brush and chisel-blend into the base color.
2. Shade above the pink areas with Prussian Blue. Wipe the brush and chisel-blend.
3. Use the liner to stipple Cadmium Yellow Light to highlight the green areas on the lower wings.

4. Accent the lower wings above the pink areas with the liner and Cobalt Turquoise. Accent the outer edges of the forewings and hind wings as shown on the Painting Worksheet.
5. Use the liner to stipple a line of thinned Ivory Black between the pink and turquoise areas.
6. Use the liner to highlight the pink areas with stippled Titanium White. Wipe the brush and stipple-blend.
7. Add touches of Titanium White to the turquoise areas with the liner.
8. Use the liner to add touches of Cadmium Yellow Light to the outer edges of the lower wings.

Exotic Butterfly Painting Worksheet

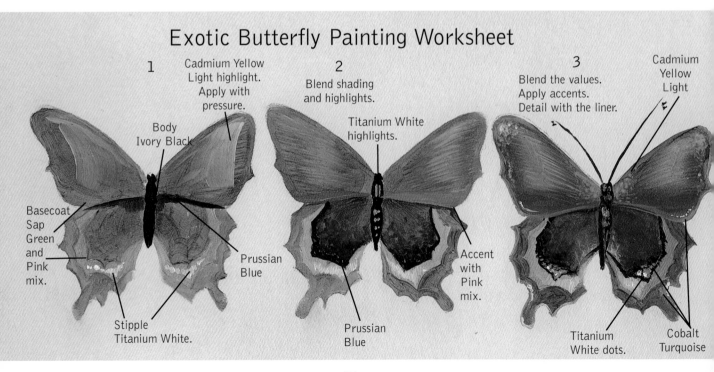

1
Cadmium Yellow Light highlight. Apply with pressure.
Body Ivory Black
Basecoat Sap Green and Pink mix.
Stipple Titanium White.
Prussian Blue

2
Blend shading and highlights.
Titanium White highlights.
Accent with Pink mix.
Prussian Blue

3
Blend the values. Apply accents. Detail with the liner.
Cadmium Yellow Light
Titanium White dots.
Cobalt Turquoise

9. Use the liner to stipple Cadmium Yellow Light highlights on the wings next to the body.

Body & Antennae:

1. Basecoat the body with the liner and thinned Ivory Black.
2. Highlight the body with stippled dots of Titanium White. Wipe the brush and stipple-blend.
3. Paint the antennae with the liner and thinned Pink mix. (*Note: Antennae are dark on the worksheet to show placement.*)

FINISHING

Gold Line & Edging:

1. Place the saucer in the center of the bowl. Hold it in place as you trace around the rim with the gold leafing adhesive pen. Lift the saucer and apply the leaf as described in "Metal Leafing."
2. Use the gold leafing adhesive pen to apply adhesive to the rim. Apply leaf as described in "Metal Leafing."

Varnish:

1. Let the painting dry for at least ten days.
2. Apply five to ten coats of spray varnish, drying to the touch after each coat.

Pattern for Exotic Butterfly

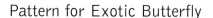

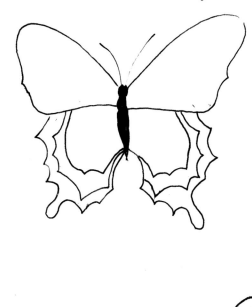

Pattern for Bromeliad Stencil

Peacock Butterfly Canvas

This canvas is a harmonious union of surface texture, decoupage techniques, and oil painting. Paper with script writing was decoupaged directly to the canvas, while a stenciled section adds a bold design element to the piece. The bold colors and striking design of the wings make the butterfly seem vividly alive.

SUPPLIES

Painting Surface

Pre-Stretched Canvas, 6" x 10"

Oil Palette

Burnt Sienna

Burnt Umber

Cadmium Red Medium

Cadmium Yellow Light

Ivory Black

Titanium White

Ultramarine Blue

Brushes

Bright – #4, #8

Flat Shader – #2, #10, #12

Short Liner – 10/0

Wash – ¾"

Acrylic Background Colors

Gold Metallic

Ivory Black

Raw Sienna

Titanium White

Other Supplies

Moldeling Paste

Stencil – Leaf or Plume Design

Natural Sponge

Decoupage Medium/Glue

Papers with lettering for decoupage

Acrylic ink–Burnt Umber, Super Black

Masking Tape

PREPARATION

Prepare the Surface:

Prepare the canvas, following the instructions in the "Surfaces" section of the "Supplies" chapter.

Apply the Background Elements:

1. Apply a parchment finish over the entire canvas, following the instructions in the "General Information and Techniques" section. Let dry.
2. Measure 1" from the top and draw a very light pencil line. Paint a band of Ivory Black acrylic. Let dry.
3. Measure 5" from the bottom of the black band and draw a very light pencil line. Cut a 1" strip of lettered paper the width of the canvas. Decoupage the strip of paper to the canvas, following the instructions in the "General Information and Techniques" section. Let dry.
4. Measure and tape off 5" down from the bottom of the paper strip. Paint with Ivory Black acrylic. Let dry.
5. Cut a strip of paper to cover the remaining area on the bottom of the canvas. Decoupage the strip of paper to the canvas, following the instructions in the "General Information and Techniques" section. Let dry.

Stencil the Texture:

1. Pour a small amount of Gold Metallic acrylic onto the palette.
2. Pick up a little paint with the sponge and pounce on the palette. Tap on a paper towel to remove excess paint.
3. Position the stencil and hold it in place.
4. Pounce the sponge lightly over the stencil. Expect imperfections—they are part of the charm. Carefully remove the stencil.
5. Reposition the stencil and continue to add leaves/plumes to the black area. Let dry. Remove the tape.

Decoupage:

1. Decoupage lettered paper on the canvas below the stenciled area. Let dry.
2. Trace and transfer the butterfly.

Color Mixes:

Premix the following oil colors with a palette knife:
- Dark Orange: equal parts Burnt Sienna + Cadmium Red Medium
- Ice Blue: equal parts Ultramarine Blue + Titanium White

Continued on page 38

Continued from page 36

PAINT THE BUTTERFLY

See the Peacock Butterfly Painting Worksheet.

Basecoat the Wings & Body:

1. Basecoat the brown sections of the wing with Burnt Umber.
2. Basecoat the orange sections of the wing with the Dark Orange mix.
3. Basecoat the blue sections with the Ice Blue mix.
4. Basecoat the black sections with Ivory Black.
5. Basecoat the yellow sections with Cadmium Yellow Light.
6. Basecoat the body with Burnt Umber.

Wings:

1. Use the liner to shade the orange areas with stippled Burnt Umber. Wipe the liner and tap to soften.
2. Use a bright brush to apply a Cadmium Yellow Light highlight to the orange areas on the forewings and the hind wings. Wipe the brush and chisel-blend.
3. Use the liner and thinned Titanium White + Cadmium Yellow Light to apply brighter highlights to the orange areas.
4. Using the chisel edge of the #4 bright brush, wiggle slightly to blend where colors meet. Wipe the brush frequently.

5. Use the liner to add dots of the Ice Blue mix to the orange areas of the forewings as shown on the Painting Worksheet. Add Ice Blue mix accents to the lower outer edges of the forewings.
6. Use the liner to stipple Titanium White onto the blue "eye" areas. Wipe the liner and stipple-blend to soften. Add tiny strokes of Titanium White to the blue dots and accents.
7. Use the liner to stipple Titanium White onto the yellow areas. Wipe the liner and stipple-blend to soften.
8. Detail the dark sections with dots of Titanium White + Cadmium Yellow Light.
9. Use the liner and Ivory Black to clean up any uneven lines on the wing edges.

Body & Antennae:

1. Use the liner to stipple Titanium White onto the center of the body. Wipe the brush and stipple-blend to soften.
2. Add small segments to the body with the liner and Titanium White. Stipple-blend.
3. Paint the antennae with the liner and thinned Burnt Umber.

FINISHING

1. Let the painting dry for at least ten days.
2. Apply five to ten coats of spray varnish, drying to the touch after each coat.

Peacock Butterfly Painting Worksheet

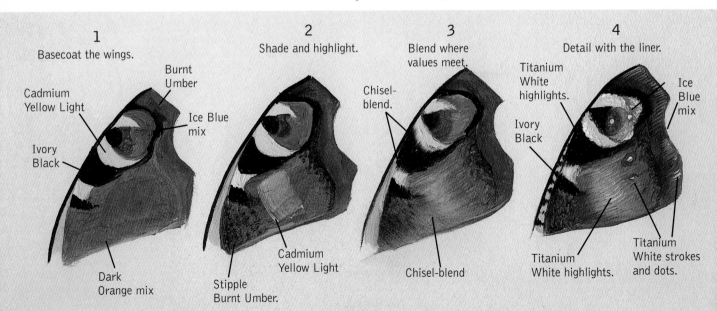

1 Basecoat the wings.
Cadmium Yellow Light — Burnt Umber — Ice Blue mix — Ivory Black — Dark Orange mix

2 Shade and highlight.
Cadmium Yellow Light — Stipple Burnt Umber.

3 Blend where values meet.
Chisel-blend. — Chisel-blend

4 Detail with the liner.
Titanium White highlights. — Ivory Black — Ice Blue mix — Titanium White highlights. — Titanium White strokes and dots.

Pattern for Peacock Butterfly

Pattern for Vanessa

Instructions begin on page 40.

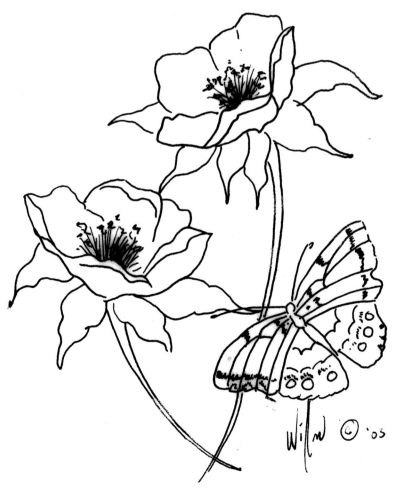

Vanessa

SUPPLIES

Painting Surfaces
Wooden bowl, 8" diameter
Penholder with wooden base

Oil Palette
Burnt Umber
Cadmium Red Medium
Cadmium Yellow Light
Ivory Black
Titanium White
Ultramarine Blue

Brushes
Bright – #4, #8
Flat Shader – #2, #10, #12
Short Liner – 10/0
Wash – ¾"

Acrylic Background Colors
Gold Metallic
Titanium White
Brilliant Ultramarine

Other Supplies
Stencil – Scrollwork Pattern
Variegated Metal Leaf
Metal Leaf Sealer and Adhesive

This wooden bowl and penholder make a beautiful set for a lady's desk. Together, butterflies and flowers illustrate how nature's living things depend upon each other. To unify the combination of design elements, it's important for colors to flow throughout the design from one element to another.

PREPARATION

Prepare the Surface:
1. Remove the metal penholder from the wooden base.
2. Prepare the wood surfaces, following the instructions in the "Surfaces" section of the "Supplies" chapter.

Basecoat the Surfaces:
1. Mix Ice Blue acrylic: equal parts Brilliant Ultramarine acrylic + Titanium White acrylic. Using the wash brush, basecoat the wood surfaces with several coats. Let dry, and sand after each coat.
2. Trace and transfer the pattern.

Stencil the Penholder:
1. Position the stencil and hold it in place around the rim.
2. Stencil design with Titanium White. Gently lift the stencil from the surface. Let dry.
3. Accent the scrollwork with a liner and thinned Gold Metallic acrylic.

Metal Leaf the Bowl
1. Apply variegated metal leaf to the bowl rim, following instructions under "Metal Leafing."

Color Mixes:
Premix the following oil color values with a palette knife:
• Orange: 3 parts Cadmium Yellow Light + 1 part Cadmium Red Medium
• Medium Green: 5 parts Cadmium Yellow Light + 1 part Ivory Black + a touch of Titanium White
• Dark Green: 3 parts Medium Green + 1 part Ivory Black
• Light Green: 2 parts Medium Green + 1 part Titanium White

PAINT THE BUTTERFLY

See the Vanessa Painting Worksheet.

Basecoat the Wings & Body:
1. Basecoat the wings with the Orange value. As you paint over the transferred lines, use the stylus to draw the segment lines so you can see where to place the shading and highlights.
2. Basecoat the section on the lower wings near the body with Burnt Umber.
3. Use the liner to add the Burnt Umber markings to the wings.
4. Basecoat the body with Burnt Umber.
5. Use the liner to add Ultramarine Blue dots to the wings.

Continued on page 42

Continued from page 40

Shade & Highlight:

1. Use the liner and Cadmium Yellow Light to stipple dots of color close to the outer edge of each segment. Wipe the liner and stipple-blend into the base color. Allow the brush to travel in and out of the values, softly connecting the colors.
2. Using the liner, apply Cadmium Red Medium to each segment on the edge nearest to the body. Wipe the brush and stipple-blend toward the middle of the segment.
3. To blend the Burnt Umber into the Orange value on the lower wing, place the chisel edge of the #4 bright brush where the colors meet and wiggle the brush from side to side, connecting the two colors. If the color becomes muddy, wipe the brush and continue.
4. Use the liner and Cadmium Yellow Light to highlight the center of the thorax and the segments of the abdomen. Start in the brightest area and stipple out toward the edge.

Add Details:

1. Paint the segment lines with the liner and thinned Ivory Black.
2. Mix equal parts Burnt Umber + Ivory Black. Thin the mix and use the liner to paint the remainder of the dark markings on the butterfly. Reload the liner, as needed, to keep the color rich and dark.
3. Use the liner to highlight the blue wing dots with stippled dots of Titanium White.
4. Use the liner and Titanium White to paint white markings on the edges of the wings and within the orange sections of the upper wings. Reload each time you paint a spot.
5. Streak highlights in the middle of the wing sections with the liner and Titanium White.
6. Paint the antennae with the liner and thinned Burnt Umber.

PAINT THE LEAVES

See the Vanessa Painting Worksheet.

Leaves & Stem:

1. Basecoat the leaves and stem with the Medium Green value. As you paint over the transferred lines, use the stylus to draw lines where the leaves overlap so you can see where to place the shading and highlights.
2. Apply the Dark Green value near the flower petals, where one leaf overlaps another, and at the top of the stem under the leaves.

3. Wipe the brush. Apply the Light Green value on the very tip of each leaf.
4. Pat-blend green values where one value meets with another.
5. Using the liner and Cadmium Yellow Light, apply a thin line to the edge where one leaf overlaps another.
6. With the #4 bright brush and the Orange value, add accents to a few of the leaves. Apply the accents sparingly, wipe the brush, and pat-blend.

PAINT THE FLOWERS

See the Vanessa Painting Worksheet.

Petals:

1. Basecoat each petal with the #4 bright brush and Titanium White.
2. Shade with the #4 bright brush and a touch of the Medium Green value. Apply the shading underneath a turned petal and near the center of the flower. Wipe the brush and pat-blend.
3. Use the liner and thinned Titanium White to highlight any flipped sections of the petals that have disappeared or that are too dark.

Stamens:

1. Apply a little of the Orange value in the flower center at the base of the stamens.
2. Wipe the brush. Apply the stamen color with choppy strokes of Cadmium Yellow Light. Wipe the brush and blend the orange into the yellow.
3. Using the liner and thinned Cadmium Yellow Light, paint thin yellow stamen lines coming from the center of the flower.
4. Pick up a blob of Cadmium Yellow Light on the tip of the liner and add dots on the stamens. Reload the brush for each dot.
5. Add a few Orange value dots with the liner.
6. Pick up a blob of Titanium White on the tip of the liner and add more dots. Reload the brush for each dot.

Accents:

Pick up Orange value with the #4 bright brush. Wipe most of the paint off on a paper towel so it doesn't overpower the white petals. Touch to the edge of a few of the petals, wipe the brush, and blend.

FINISHING

1. Let the painting dry for at least ten days.
2. Apply five to ten coats of spray varnish, drying to the touch after each coat.
3. Replace the metal penholder in the wooden base.

Vanessa Painting Worksheet

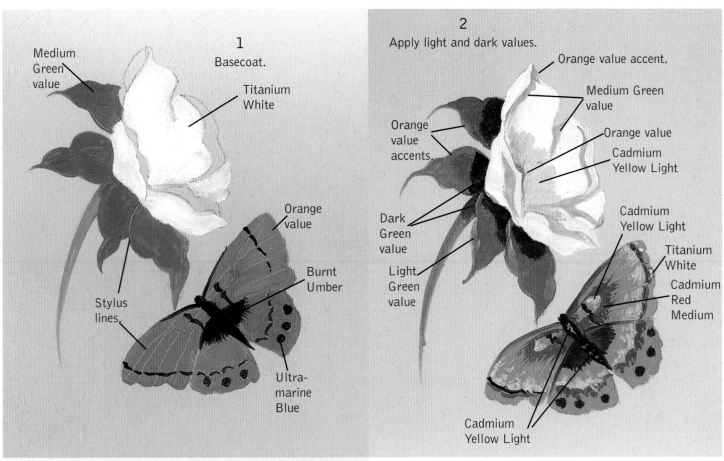

1
Basecoat.

Medium Green value

Titanium White

Orange value

Burnt Umber

Stylus lines.

Ultra-marine Blue

2
Apply light and dark values.

Orange value accent.

Medium Green value

Orange value accents.

Orange value

Cadmium Yellow Light

Dark Green value

Light Green value

Cadmium Yellow Light

Titanium White

Cadmium Red Medium

Cadmium Yellow Light

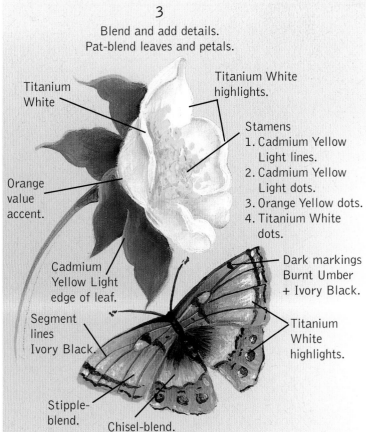

3
Blend and add details.
Pat-blend leaves and petals.

Titanium White

Titanium White highlights.

Stamens
1. Cadmium Yellow Light lines.
2. Cadmium Yellow Light dots.
3. Orange Yellow dots.
4. Titanium White dots.

Orange value accent.

Cadmium Yellow Light edge of leaf.

Segment lines Ivory Black.

Dark markings Burnt Umber + Ivory Black.

Titanium White highlights.

Stipple-blend.

Chisel-blend.

43

Pink Orchids & Butterfly

Exotic orchids remind me of romance, drama, and passion. With their range of shapes and colors, they are fascinating flowers to paint. Pat-blending gives the petals their silky smoothness; stipple-blending gives the butterfly wings their iridescent effect.

SUPPLIES

Painting Surface
Masonite panel, 4" x 8"

Oil Palette
Alizarin Crimson
Cadmium Yellow Light
Cadmium Red Medium
Dioxazine Purple
Ivory Black
Magenta
Raw Sienna
Sap Green
Titanium White

Brushes
Bright – #4, #8
Flat Shader – #2, #10, #12
Short Liner – 10/0
Wash – ¾"

Acrylic Background Colors
Crimson Alizarin
Magenta
Raw Sienna
Titanium White

Other Supplies
Modeling or Texture Paste
Stencil – Renaissance Corners & Borders
Plate–to use as a template
Metal Leaf Adhesive Pen

PREPARATION

Stencil the Texture:
1. Position the stencil and hold it in place. Leave unstenciled areas for painting the design.
2. Use a palette knife to texture paste or modeling paste over the stencil. Gently lift the stencil from the surface. Let dry.
3. Refer to project photo for placement.

Basecoat the Surface:
1. Mix Warm White acrylic: Titanium White acrylic + touch of Raw Sienna acrylic. Using the ¾" wash brush, basecoat the surface, including the stenciled texture. Let dry.
2. Mix Pink acrylic: 1 part Magenta acrylic + 1 part Titanium White acrylic.
3. Basecoat the surface again with Warm White acrylic mix. While the paint is wet, pick up touches of Crimson Alizarin acrylic, Raw Sienna acrylic, and the Pink acrylic mix. Softly slip-slap into the background. Wipe the brush frequently and continue to work the colors into the light background. Let dry. *Note:* The darker slip-slapped pink is done with oil later; you are simply getting the creamy pink base.
4. Referring to the photo for placement, lay the plate over the panel. With a pencil, lightly trace an arc to divide the background.
5. Trace and transfer the pattern.

Color Mixes:
Premix the following oil color values with a palette knife:
• Medium Pink: 1 part Magenta + 1 part Titanium White + a touch of Alizarin Crimson
• Dark Pink: 1 part Magenta + 1 part Alizarin Crimson
• Pink Shade: Magenta + a touch of Dioxazine Purple
• Light Pink: equal parts Titanium White + Medium Pink Mix

PAINT THE ORCHIDS

See the Pink Orchids & Butterfly Painting Worksheet.
Petals:
1. Basecoat each petal with the Light Pink value.

Continued on page 46

Continued from page 44

2. Shade with the Medium Pink value near the flower center and where petals overlap. Wipe the brush and blend to streak the shading into the middle area of the petal.
3. Using Titanium White, highlight the tops of the petals and the edges of petals that lie on top of a petal below. Wipe the brush and blend the white into the middle area of the petal.
4. Deepen shading, where needed, with the Pink Shade value. Stroke to blend.
5. Highlight with the liner and Titanium White.

Centers:

1. Basecoat the yellow areas with a mixture of Cadmium Yellow Light + a touch of Titanium White.
2. Apply Dark Pink value to the dark areas.
3. Use the liner to stipple-blend between the yellow and dark pink areas.
4. Highlight the very center of the throat with the liner and Titanium White.
5. Deepen the shading with the liner and Dark Pink value.
6. Add accent dots with the liner and Dark Pink value.

Veins & Details:

1. Thin Dark Pink value to the consistency of ink. Use the liner to suggest the veins in the petals.
2. Outline some of the petal edges with the liner and thinned Titanium White.
3. Tap a few Titanium White dots with the liner to accent the petals. Refer to the Painting Worksheet for placement.
4. Add some Cadmium Yellow Light accents in the highlight areas. Wipe the brush and pat-blend.

Stems & Buds:

1. Mix 3 parts Cadmium Yellow Light + 1 part Ivory Black + 1 part Sap Green + a touch of Titanium White. Basecoat the stems and buds.
2. Use the liner to highlight with Cadmium Yellow Light. Wipe the liner and gently stipple-blend to soften.
3. Shade the stems and buds with the green basecoat mix + a touch of Ivory Black. Wipe the brush and blend.
4. Use the liner to highlight with Titanium White. Wipe the brush and stipple-blend.
5. Apply the lightest highlights with the liner and Titanium White.

Continued on page 48

Pink Orchids & Butterfly Painting Worksheet

Orchid

1

Basecoat the petals with Light Pink value.

Apply the values.

Cadmium Yellow Light + Titanium White

Titanium White

Dark Pink value

Medium Pink value

2

Pat-blend the values.

Dark Pink value

Cadmium Yellow Light accents.

Dark Pink value

3

Detail with the liner.

Titanium White dots.

Veins Thinned Dark Pink.

Titanium White

Bud & Butterfly

1

Basecoat and apply the values.

Basecoat Cadmium Yellow Light.

2

Blend.

Titanium White

Stipple Alizarin Crimson.

Highlight.

Shade.

3

Chisel-blend.

Stipple-blend.

4

Stipple Titanium White highlight.

Blend the values.

Lines and details Dark Pink value.

Titanium White highlights.

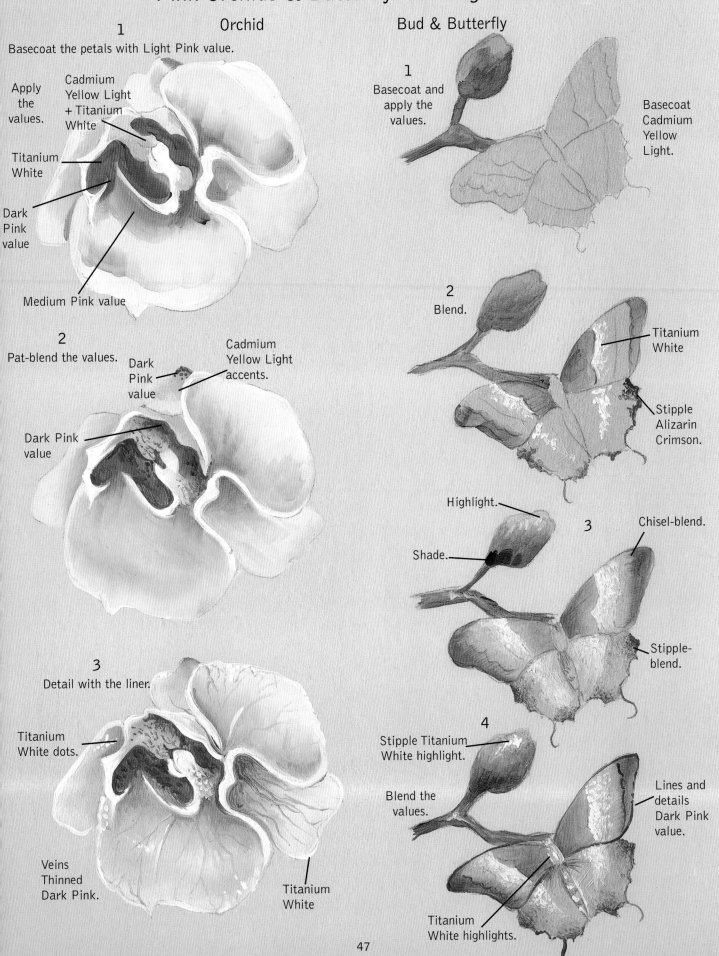

Continued from page 46

PAINT THE BUTTERFLY

See the Pink Orchids & Butterfly Painting Worksheet.

Wings & Body:

1. Basecoat the wings and body with Cadmium Yellow Light.
2. Add Cadmium Red Medium to the inner and outer areas of the forewings. Wipe the brush and chisel-blend.
3. Use the liner to stipple Alizarin Crimson on the hind wings. Wipe the brush and stipple-blend.
4. Chisel-blend the orange into the yellow on the forewings.
5. Use the liner to stipple Titanium White highlights on the wings. Wipe the brush and stipple-blend.
6. Shade the body with the liner and Cadmium Red Medium. Wipe the brush and stipple-blend.
7. Use the liner to stipple accents of Alizarin Crimson on the darkest outer parts of the orange-stippled shading on the hind wings. Stipple-blend into the orange.
8. Use the liner and Titanium White to stipple the brightest highlights on the wings.

Details:

1. Paint the body segment lines with the liner and thinned Titanium White.
2. Use the liner and thinned Alizarin Crimson to line the wings and paint the wing details.
3. Use the liner and thinned Cadmium Red Medium to pull the hair-like lines from the thorax out over the hind wings.
4. Paint the antennae with the liner and thinned Cadmium Red Medium.

FINISHING

Background:

1. Using the #8 bright brush and the pink values, slip-slap the pink portion of the background. Do not overblend. Let dry.
2. Create the arc dividing the two areas with the metal leaf adhesive pen. Replace the plate and use its rim as a template. Apply metal leaf, following the instructions under "Metal Leafing."

Varnish:

1. Let the painting dry for at least ten days.
2. Apply five to ten coats of spray varnish, drying to the touch after each coat.

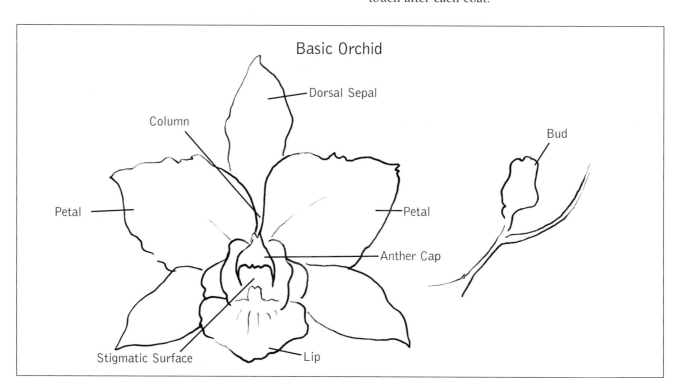

Basic Orchid

Dorsal Sepal

Column

Bud

Petal

Petal

Anther Cap

Stigmatic Surface

Lip

Pattern for Pink Orchids & Butterfly

Chickadee & Cherries

SUPPLIES

Painting Surface
Canvas, 10" x 10"

Oil Palette
Alizarin Crimson
Burnt Sienna
Burnt Umber
Cadmium Red Medium
Cadmium Yellow Light
Ivory Black
Raw Sienna
Titanium White
Ultramarine Blue

Brushes
Bright – #4, #8
Flat Shader – #2, #10, #12
Short Liner – 10/0, 18/0
Wash – ¾"

Acrylic Background Colors
Raw Sienna
Titanium White

Other Supplies
High-Density Foam Roller, 4"

Tiny chickadees look delicate, but they are amazingly strong and hardy. The rich reds of the cherries provide a warm contrast for the neat black-and-white feathers of this curious little fellow. Place the highlights on the cherries opposite the darkest shading.

PREPARATION

Prepare the Surface:
Prepare the canvas, following the instructions in the "Surfaces" section of the "Supplies" chapter.

Apply the Eggshell Finish Background:
1. Mix Warm White acrylic: Titanium White acrylic + a touch of Raw Sienna acrylic. Drizzle on the canvas and spread with the foam roller. Add paint and roll until the surface is evenly covered. Let dry.
2. Rub the surface with a piece of brown paper bag to smooth. Remove sanding dust.
3. Roll on another coat of the Warm White acrylic mix. Let dry.
4. Trace and lightly transfer the design.

Color Mixes:
Premix the following oil color values with a palette knife:
- #1 – Orange: 1 part Cadmium Yellow Light + 3 parts Cadmium Red Medium
- #2 – Brown: 1 part Burnt Umber + 1 part Titanium White + a touch of Ivory Black
- #3 – Light Green: equal parts Medium Green value + Cadmium Yellow Light
- #4 – Medium Green: 5 parts Cadmium Yellow Light + 1 part Ivory Black + a touch of Titanium White
- #5 – Dark Green: Medium Green value + a touch of Ivory Black

PAINT THE CHICKADEE

See the Chickadee Painting Worksheet.
Eye:
1. Thin a mix of Burnt Umber + Titanium White to an inky consistency. Using the liner, paint a line around the pupil. This line should be thicker at the back of the eye.
2. Paint the pupil with the liner and thinned Ivory Black. Adjust the shape of the eye if necessary, rounding it out or widening it.

Continued on page 52

COLOR MIXES   #1   #2   #3   #4   #5

Continued from page 50

Head:

1. Basecoat the cheek with Titanium White.
2. Shade the cheek with Raw Sienna. Wipe the brush and chisel-blend.
3. Basecoat the crown and throat with Ivory Black.
4. Connect the crown and throat with the cheek by setting the chisel edge of the brush where the two colors meet and wiggling it slightly between the colors.
5. Load the liner with Titanium White. Highlight the feathers above the beak and across the crown, the throat, and the cheek with small, light strokes. Begin the strokes near the beak and follow the growth pattern and the curve of the head. *I use a short liner and load the brush like it's a flat brush with Titanium White. This is what I use to highlight the feathers above the beak, on the cheek, and at the neck. You will have to reload the liner every few strokes.*
6. Basecoat the beak with the liner and slightly thinned Burnt Umber.
7. Wipe the brush. Highlight down the center of the beak with Titanium White.

Breast:

1. Basecoat the breast with Titanium White.
2. Shade the breast with Raw Sienna. Wipe the brush and chisel-blend.
3. Deepen shading under the throat, wings, and tail with Burnt Umber. Wipe the brush and chisel-blend.
4. Accent with touches of Burnt Sienna. Wipe the brush and chisel-blend.
5. Brighten the highlight on the front of the breast with the liner and Titanium White.

Toes:

1. Use the liner to basecoat the toes with Ivory Black.
2. Tap a touch of Titanium White over the toes with the liner to highlight. Wipe the brush and stipple-blend.

Wings & Tail:

1. Basecoat the wings and tail with the Brown value. As you paint over the transferred lines, use the stylus to draw the edge of the feather so you can see where to place the shading and highlights.
2. Paint the feather lines with the #4 bright brush and Titanium White. Starting at the tip of the feather, draw the line with the chisel edge in one continuous movement.

3. Shade under each feather line and at the base of the feathers with a tiny bit of Burnt Umber. Wipe the brush and chisel-blend.
4. Using Titanium White, add small strokes, following the curve of the shoulder over the wing. Wipe the brush and chisel-blend into the base color.
5. Wipe the brush and chisel-blend to soften the transition between the cheek and the shoulder.

Shading & Highlights:

1. Strengthen the shading where needed, blending softly between values.
2. Using the liner and Titanium White, place a dot to highlight the eye.
3. Add tiny dots to highlight the eye ring, as shown on the Painting Worksheet.
4. Add tiny dots of Titanium White to highlight the beak.
5. With the liner and Titanium White, highlight the throat under the beak. Strengthen the highlight on the crown.

Continued on page 54

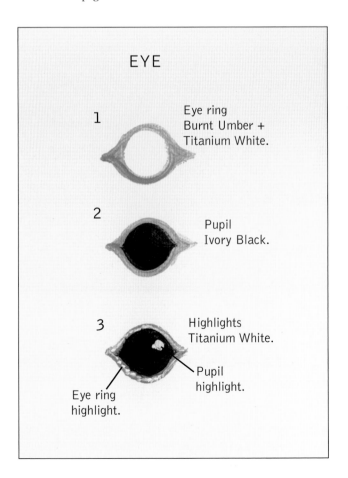

EYE

1 Eye ring
   Burnt Umber +
   Titanium White.

2 Pupil
   Ivory Black.

3 Highlights
   Titanium White.

   Pupil
   highlight.

Eye ring
highlight.

Chickadee Painting Worksheet

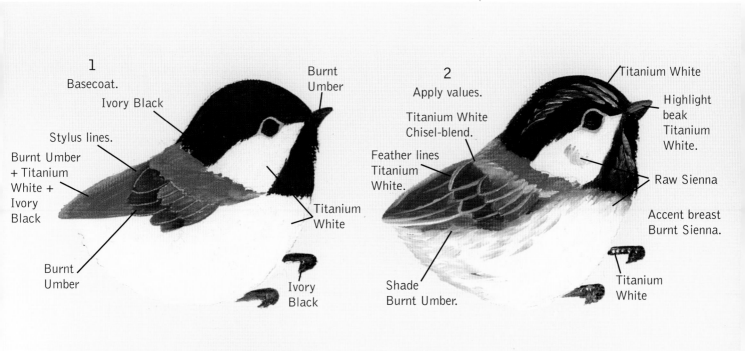

1
Basecoat.

Ivory Black

Stylus lines.

Burnt Umber
+ Titanium
White +
Ivory
Black

Burnt
Umber

Burnt
Umber

Titanium
White

Ivory
Black

2
Apply values.

Titanium White
Chisel-blend.

Feather lines
Titanium
White.

Shade
Burnt Umber.

Titanium White

Highlight
beak
Titanium
White.

Raw Sienna

Accent breast
Burnt Sienna.

Titanium
White

3
Blend the values.
Chisel-blend the feathers.

Chisel-blend.

Chisel-
blend.

Stipple-
blend.

4
Deepen shading.
Brighten highlights.
Continue blending.
Detail with the liner.

Highlight
Titanium White.

Titanium
White

Continued from page 52

PAINT THE CHERRIES & LEAVES

Cherries:

See the Cherry Painting Worksheet.

1. Mix Alizarin Crimson + a touch of Ivory Black. Apply the dark value choppily in a crescent-shaped shadow. Leave a line at the edge of selected cherries for a reflected light.

2. Using the same brush and color, shade where one cherry is behind another or under a leaf.

3. Fill in the remainder of the cherry with Cadmium Red Medium, including the edge left for reflected light. Connect the dark and medium values with choppy pat-blending.

4. Use the liner to tap in Cadmium Yellow Light highlights where light would hit the cherry, opposite the crescent shadow. Stipple-blend to soften.

5. Add an accent line to the side of the cherry that overlaps another design element, using the liner and thinned Ultramarine Blue + Titanium White.

6. Paint all of the cherries. Deepen shading and brighten highlights, blending softly where values meet.

7. Add the final highlight with the liner and a few dots of Titanium White.

Leaves & Stems:

1. Apply the Dark Green value at the base of the leaf, down the center vein line, and on the shaded areas of the stem.

2. Paint the rest of the leaf and stem with the Medium Green value. Pat-blend.

3. Using the chisel edge of the brush, streak from the vein line out toward the edge of the leaf.

4. Apply the Light Green value to the edges of some of the leaves, pat-blend, and then streak the light value back into the leaf toward the center with the chisel edge of the brush.

5. Using the liner and the Medium Green value, stroke a highlight on the top curve of the stem that goes to the final cherry.

PAINT THE BUTTERFLY

See the Butterfly Painting Worksheet.

Basecoat the Wings & Body:

1. Basecoat the wings with the Orange value.

2. Basecoat the dark areas on the wings near the body with Burnt Umber. Apply Burnt Umber to shade where one wing is behind another.

3. Chisel-blend to join the values.

4. Basecoat the body with the liner and Burnt Umber.

Shade & Highlight:

1. Use Cadmium Yellow Light to apply highlight strokes to the wings. Wipe the brush and chisel-blend.

2. Using the liner and Cadmium Yellow Light, stroke a highlight on the leading edges of the forewings and the top and bottom edges of the visible hind wing.

3. Highlight the center of the thorax and the lower abdomen with the liner and Cadmium Yellow Light. Stipple-blend.

4. Strengthen highlights and shading. Chisel-blend.

Add Details:

1. Mix equal parts Burnt Umber + Ivory Black. Thin the mix and use the liner to paint the dark markings on the wings and the outer edges of the wings. Reload the liner, as needed, to keep the color rich and dark.

2. Use the liner and Titanium White to paint the brightest highlights on the wings. Wipe the brush and stipple-blend.

3. Paint the antennae with the liner and thinned Burnt Umber. Start the antennae from the butterfly's head and gently lift the pressure on the brush as you stroke.

FINISHING

1. Let the painting dry for at least ten days.

2. Apply five to ten coats of spray varnish, drying to the touch after each coat.

Cherry Painting Worksheet

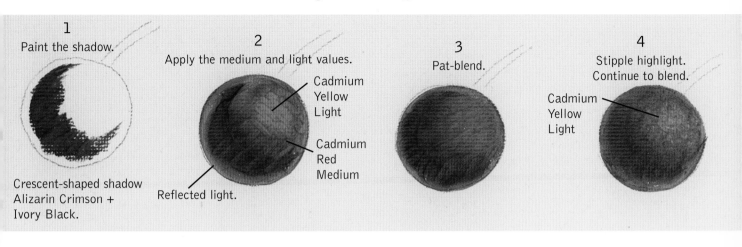

1
Paint the shadow.

Crescent-shaped shadow
Alizarin Crimson +
Ivory Black.

2
Apply the medium and light values.

Cadmium
Yellow
Light

Cadmium
Red
Medium

Reflected light.

3
Pat-blend.

4
Stipple highlight.
Continue to blend.

Cadmium
Yellow
Light

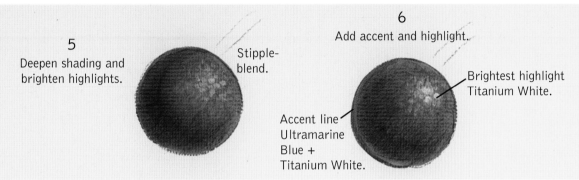

5
Deepen shading and
brighten highlights.

Stipple-
blend.

6
Add accent and highlight.

Brightest highlight
Titanium White.

Accent line
Ultramarine
Blue +
Titanium White.

Butterfly Painting Worksheet

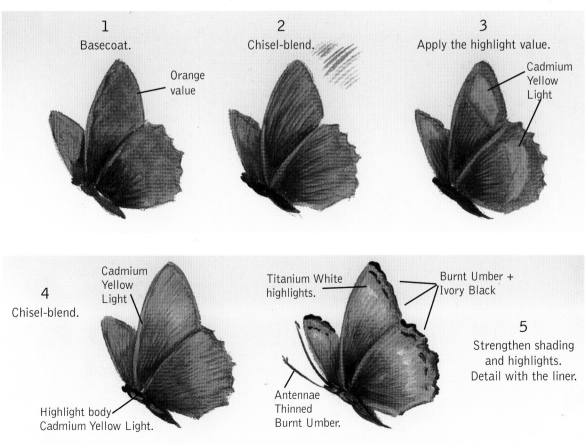

1
Basecoat.

Orange
value

2
Chisel-blend.

3
Apply the highlight value.

Cadmium
Yellow
Light

4
Chisel-blend.

Cadmium
Yellow
Light

Highlight body
Cadmium Yellow Light.

Titanium White
highlights.

Burnt Umber +
Ivory Black

5
Strengthen shading
and highlights.
Detail with the liner.

Antennae
Thinned
Burnt Umber.

Pattern for Chickadee & Cherries

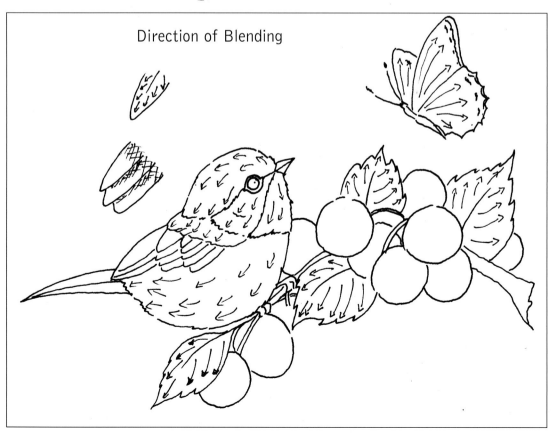

Direction of Blending

Pattern for Baby Ducks

Instructions begin on page 58.

Blending Direction & Shading Diagram

Baby Ducks

SUPPLIES

Painting Surface
Canvas, 10" x 10"

Oil Palette
Burnt Sienna
Burnt Umber
Cadmium Red Medium
Cadmium Yellow Light
Ivory Black
Raw Sienna
Sap Green
Titanium White
Ultramarine Blue
Yellow Ochre

Brushes
Bright – #4, #8
Flat Shader – #2, #10, #12
Filbert Grainer – ⅜"
Grainer – ⅜"
Short Liner – 10/0
Wash – ¾"
Lunar Blender – ⅜"

Acrylic Background Colors
Titanium White
Yellow Ochre

When I painted these fluffy little babies, I envisioned them in a room shared by children and their siblings. There is nothing cuter than baby ducks! You can almost imagine them getting ready to leap from their nest into the water below. Their soft down is easy to paint with a grainer, a brush that makes multiple marks with a single stroke.

PREPARATION

Prepare the Surface:
Prepare the canvas, following the instructions in the "Surfaces" section.

Basecoat the Surface:
1. Mix equal parts Yellow Ochre acrylic + Titanium White acrylic. Basecoat the canvas, using the wash brush. Let dry.
2. Apply a second coat, if needed, for opaque coverage. Let dry.
3. Trace and transfer the design.

Color Mixes:
Premix the following oil color values with a palette knife:
• Dark Brown: equal parts Burnt Umber + Ivory Black
• Highlight Yellow: equal parts Cadmium Yellow Light + Titanium White
• Light Yellow: equal parts Cadmium Yellow Light + Yellow Ochre
• Medium Yellow: equal parts Yellow Ochre + Raw Sienna
• Dark Yellow: Add Burnt Sienna to the Medium Yellow Mix
• Baby Pink: equal parts Cadmium Red Medium + Burnt Sienna + Titanium White

PAINT THE DUCKLINGS

See the Baby Ducks Painting Worksheet.
Eyes:
1. Thin some Light Yellow value to an inky consistency. Using a liner, paint a large line around the eye.
2. Paint the pupils with the liner and Ivory Black. Let the eye set.
3. Pick up Titanium White on the end of the liner and add the highlight dots.

Beaks:
1. Basecoat the pink portions of the beak with the Baby Pink mix.
2. Basecoat the rest of the beaks with the Dark Brown value. Wipe the brush and pat-blend.
3. Using the liner, highlight the lower beak with a thin line of Titanium White.
4. Using the liner, apply a highlight on the upper pink section with the Baby Pink value + more Titanium White. Tap over the highlight to soften.

5. Add a dot of highlight on the upper beak with the liner and thinned Titanium White.

6. Highlight around the nostril with the liner and Titanium White. Wipe the brush and stipple-blend to soften.

7. Add a few brighter dots with the liner and Titanium White.

8. Using the liner, define the edge of the beak with a thin line of Ivory Black.

Continued on page 60

Continued from page 59

Baby Duck Down:

1. Basecoat the yellow sections with the #4 bright brush and Light Yellow value.
2. Using the chisel edge of the brush, shade with the Medium Yellow value. Wipe the brush and chisel-blend.
3. Basecoat the dark head area with the Dark Brown value. Wipe the brush and blend by wiggling the chisel edge of the brush where the two values meet.
4. Basecoat above the beak with the Dark Yellow value. Chisel-blend.
5. Use the filbert grainer to apply Dark Yellow value as shading, behind the cheek, on the chin, and under the eyes. Load the brush, wipe off excess paint, and apply softly. Continue to drybrush layers of strokes until you achieve the desired depth.
6. Further shade with Burnt Sienna.
7. Highlight the yellow sections with the grainer and Highlight Yellow value. Shade with a few strokes of Burnt Umber in darkest areas. Load the brush, wipe off excess paint, and apply softly. Continue to drybrush layers of strokes until you achieve the desired depth.
8. Highlight the dark brown areas on the head with layers of strokes with the grainer, first with Dark Yellow value, then Medium Yellow value, and finally a touch of Light Yellow value.
9. Add the brightest highlights with the liner and Titanium White.

PAINT THE TREE BARK

1. Mix 1 part Dark Brown value + 1 part Titanium White + a touch of Ultramarine Blue. Basecoat the bark.
2. Mix Titanium White + a touch of

Burnt Umber to highlight the outer edges of the nooks and crannies. Apply the highlights with a small bright brush.
3. Wipe the brush. Apply Ivory Black to shade each section of bark.
4. Use the liner and thinned Ivory Black to make squiggles and cracks in the bark. Make sure the cracks go through some of the highlighted sections as well.
5. Brighten highlights with the liner and Titanium White.
6. Add squiggly moss with a liner and thinned Sap Green.
7. Highlight the moss with the liner and a mixture of equal parts Sap Green + Cadmium Yellow Light + Titanium White.

PAINT THE HOLLOW BACKGROUND

1. Basecoat the dark hollow behind the ducklings with Ivory Black.
2. While the paint is wet, pick up the Dark Brown value and slip-slap into the black base color. Do not overblend.
3. Use the liner and Titanium White to overlay some duck down, separating the ducklings from the background.

FINISHING

1. Let the painting dry for at least ten days.
2. Apply five to ten coats of spray varnish, drying to the touch after each coat.

Baby Ducks Painting Worksheet

1

Basecoat.
Apply values with the chisel edge of the brush.
Wipe the brush and gently chisel-blend to connect.

Basecoat yellow areas Cadmium Yellow Light + Yellow Ochre.

Dark Yellow

Ivory Black

Titanium White

Baby Pink value

Shade with Medium Yellow value.

Highlight Titanium White + Cadmium Yellow Light.

Highlight Dark Yellow.

Dark Brown

Highlight Light Yellow.

Chisel-blending.

2

Soften the down with the grainer.
Thin the dark and light values.
Layer grainer strokes.

Grainer strokes.

Layer highlight Medium Yellow value.

Stipple-blend.

Dark Yellow

Titanium White highlights.

3

Use the liner to add final highlights and shading.

Layer highlight Light Yellow value.

Titanium White highlights

Line edge of beak Ivory Black.

Grainer strokes.

Further shade with Burnt Sienna, then Burnt Umber.

Baby Pink

Light Yellow

Medium Yellow

Dark Yellow

Dark Brown

Guardian Angels Plaque

I was raised in a warm, loving environment filled with fairy tales and stories of guardian angels. When I had my own child, I realized how important it is to fill our world with wonder and the possibility of magical mysteries. White hummingbirds remind me of fairies, guardian angels, and magic. Painting creates a world where all of those mysteries exist without boundaries.

SUPPLIES

Painting Surface
Arched wooden plaque

Oil Palette
Alizarin Crimson
Burnt Sienna
Cadmium Yellow Light
Ivory Black
Magenta
Sap Green
Titanium White
Ultramarine Blue

Brushes
Bright – #2, #4, #8
Flat Shader – #10, #12
Mop – ½", ¼"
Short Liner – 10/0
Wash – ¾"
Lunar Blender – ¼"

Acrylic Background Colors
Alizarin Crimson
Magenta
Raw Sienna
Sap Green
Titanium White
Ultramarine Blue
Blending medium

Other Supplies
Modeling Paste or Texture Paste
Stencil – Flourishes & Frills
Antique Gold Rub-on Metallic Paste
Gold Leaf
Extra Thick Metal Leaf Adhesive
Sealer for Metal Leaf
Power Wash

PREPARATION

Prepare the Surface:
Prepare the wood surface, following the instructions in the "Surfaces" section of the "Supplies" chapter.

Stencil the Texture:
1. Referring to the photo for placement, position the stencil and hold it in place.
2. Use a palette knife to spread modeling paste or texture paste over the stencil. Gently lift the stencil from the surface. Let dry.

Basecoat the Surface:
1. Mix Warm White acrylic: Titanium White acrylic + touch of Raw Sienna acrylic. Using the ¾" wash brush, basecoat the surface, including the stenciled texture. Let dry.
2. Apply a second coat of Warm White acrylic.
3. Place all the acrylic colors on a dry palette. While the basecoat is wet, use the wash brush to pick up touches of the different colors and slip-slap onto the surface. Continue picking up various colors and blending on the surface, using a crisscross motion until softened into the background. Use blending medium to keep the paint wet while blending. Let dry.
4. Trace and lightly transfer the pattern.

Color Mixes:
Premix the following oil color values with a palette knife:
- Pink: equal parts Magenta + Titanium White
- Blush: 5 parts Titanium White + 1 part Burnt Sienna + 1 part Alizarin Crimson
- Violet: Titanium White + a touch of Alizarin Crimson + a touch of Ultramarine Blue
- Ice Blue: equal parts Titanium White + Ultramarine Blue
- Lily Dark: 3 parts Titanium White + 1 part Magenta + 1 part Alizarin Crimson + a touch of Blush value
- Lily Medium: Titanium White + a touch of Blush value
- Green: 3 parts Titanium White + 1 part Cadmium Yellow Light + 1 part Ivory Black
- Green Dark: 2 parts Green value + 1 part Ivory Black

Continued on page 64

Continued from page 62

PAINT THE HUMMINGBIRDS

See the White Hummingbird Painting Worksheet.

Basecoat:

1. Paint the eye ring with the liner and the Blush value.
2. Paint the pupil with the liner and thinned Ivory Black.
3. Basecoat the beak with the liner and thinned Blush value.
4. Use the #4 bright brush and Titanium White to softly basecoat the head and body feathers with short, choppy strokes.
5. Mix a wash with 3 parts thinner + 1 part Titanium White. Basecoat the wings and tail.
6. Use the #4 bright brush to pull each feather from the outer edge of the wing toward the body, allowing the strokes to show.

Apply Tints & Dark Values:

1. Shade the body above and below the wing with the #2 bright brush and a touch of Sap Green. Wipe the brush and chisel-blend.
2. Load the #2 bright brush very sparsely with various colors (Sap Green, Ice Blue value, Cadmium Yellow Light, Violet value), and softly brush the color through the wings to create a translucent effect.
3. Wipe the brush. Shade the tail with Violet value. Chisel-blend to soften.
4. Using the liner and Burnt Sienna, shade the underside of the beak with a thin line.

Blend and Apply Tints:

1. Shade behind and in front of the eye with the liner and Blush value. Wipe the liner and tap over the shading to soften.
2. Blend with small strokes of the liner and Blush value to connect the beak to the head.
3. Use the liner to accent the body and head with thinned Ice Blue value and thinned Violet value.
4. Continue to softly brush color through the wings using the #2 bright brush and various colors (Sap Green, Ice Blue value, Cadmium Yellow Light, Violet value).

Highlights & Details:

1. Use the liner to highlight the pupil of the eye with a dot of Titanium White.
2. Apply a thin line of Titanium White to highlight above the line where the upper and lower beak meet.
3. Use the liner and thinned Titanium White to highlight the crown of the head, the center of the breast, and where the feathers cover the tail.
4. Add highlight strokes to the wing tops and tail feathers with the liner and thinned Titanium White.

PAINT THE LILIES

Petals:

See the Lily Painting Worksheet.

1. Basecoat the petals with the #6 bright brush and the Lily Medium value. As you paint over the separations between petals, draw a line with the stylus to mark where they meet.
2. Wipe the brush and shade petals with the Lily Dark value. Apply shading sparsely, as it is easy to overpower the pale petal color. Wipe the brush. Streak from the outer edge of the petal toward the center vein line.
3. Highlight each petal with Titanium White. Wipe the brush. Streak into the petal.
4. Add further highlights with the liner and thinned Titanium White.
5. Using Green value, sparsely apply accents to the center of the lily. Wipe the brush and chisel-blend.
6. Darken the very center of the front lily with Green value + a touch of Ivory Black. Chisel-blend into the green.

Stamens & Anthers:

1. Basecoat the stamens with the liner and thinned Green value.
2. Highlight with a thin line of Titanium White.
3. Shade with a small amount of Ivory Black. Lightly tap the shading into the green.
4. Use the liner to paint each anther (the pollen area at the top of the stamen) with a mix of equal parts Alizarin Crimson + Cadmium Yellow Light.
5. Tap highlight dots in the middle of each anther with thinned Cadmium Yellow Light.
6. Lighten the thinned Cadmium Yellow Light with Titanium White, and add the final highlight dots.

FINISHING

Background:

1. Use the ¼" lunar blender brush to apply the Green value under the lilies.
2. Wipe the brush. Touch into the green area and "rouge" outward in a circular motion to draw the color out.
3. Use a mop brush or the tip of your finger to soften further.
4. Use the liner to tap and blend a few darker shadows closest to the flower with Ivory Black or Alizarin Crimson.

Metal Leaf:

1. Let the completed painting dry for at least ten days. Remove any dust particles.
2. Spray the stencil back with spray adhesive and lay the stencil back over the textured area.
3. Apply extra thick metal leaf adhesive with a brush over the raised area. Carefully remove stencil and allow the adhesive to tack up for 1 hour. Apply gold leaf as described in "Metal Leafing." Clean stencil immediately with Power Wash.
4. Apply metal leaf sealer and allow to dry over night.
5. Re-apply the stencil. Use the lunar blender and load with Burnt Umber; wipe most of the paint from the brush. Drybrush the Burnt Umber over the raised area to stain the leafing.

Varnishing:

1. Let the gilding dry thoroughly.
2. Apply five to ten coats of spray varnish, drying to the touch after each coat.

White Hummingbird Painting Worksheet

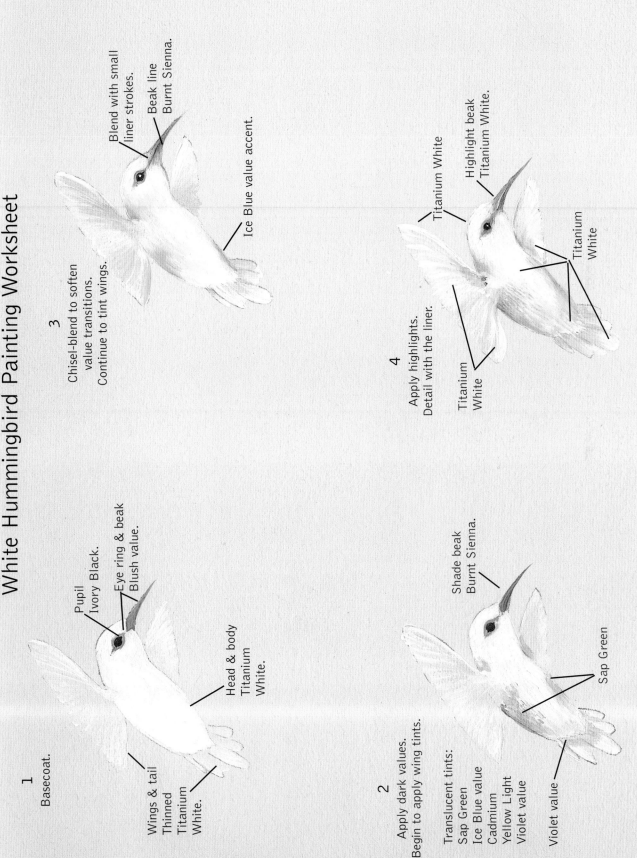

1

Basecoat.

Pupil
Ivory Black.

Eye ring & beak
Blush value.

Head & body
Titanium White.

Wings & tail
Thinned Titanium White.

2

Apply dark values.
Begin to apply wing tints.

Translucent tints:
Sap Green
Ice Blue value
Cadmium Yellow Light
Violet value

Shade beak
Burnt Sienna.

Sap Green

Violet value

3

Chisel-blend to soften value transitions.
Continue to tint wings.

Blend with small liner strokes.

Beak line
Burnt Sienna.

Ice Blue value accent.

4

Apply highlights.
Detail with the liner.

Titanium White

Highlight beak
Titanium White.

Titanium White

Titanium White

Lily Painting Worksheet

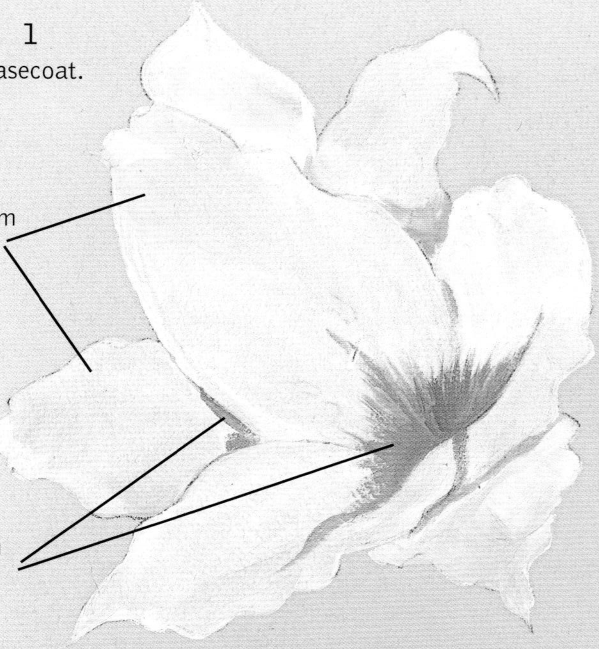

3

Chisel-blend the values.
Deepen shading.
Brighten highlights.

Highlight
Thinned
Titanium White.

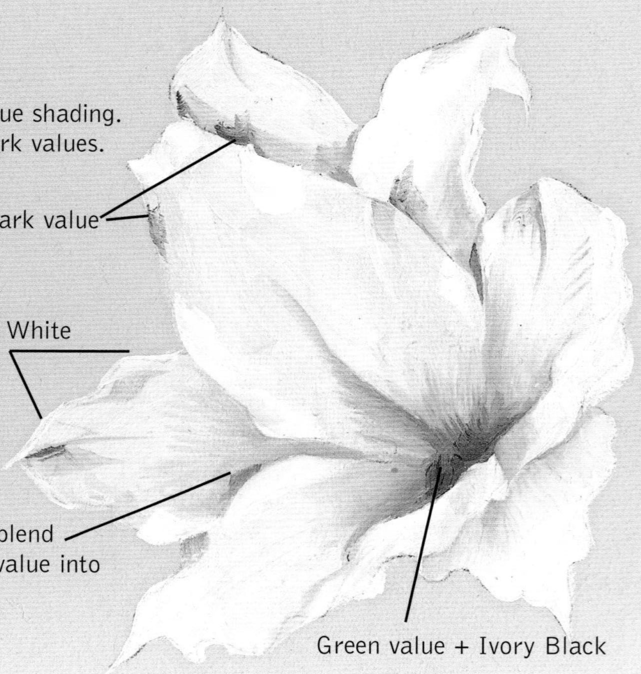

2

Blend the Green value shading.
Apply light and dark values.

Green value + Ivory Black

Lily Dark value

Titanium White

Chisel-blend
Green value into
petals.

1

Basecoat.

Lily
Medium
value

Green
value

Pattern for Guardian Angels Plaque

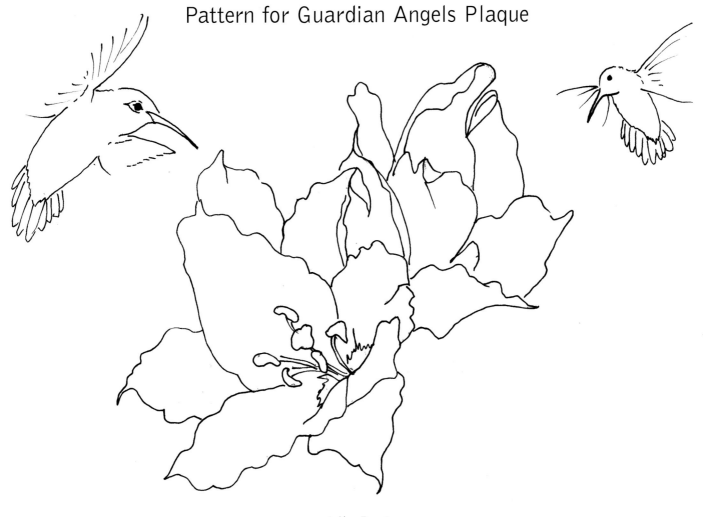

Lily Parts

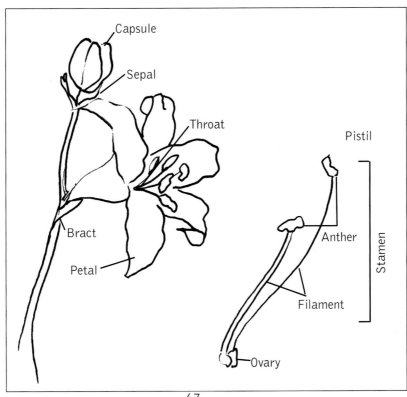

Ruby-Throated Hummingbird Journal

SUPPLIES

Painting Surface

Canvas journal, 5" x 7"

Oil Palette

Alizarin Crimson

Burnt Umber

Cadmium Yellow Light

Ivory Black

Raw Sienna

Raw Umber

Sap Green

Titanium White

Brushes

Bright – #2, #4, #8

Flat Shader – #2, #10, #12

Short Liner – 10/0

Wash – ¾"

Acrylic Background Colors

Burnt Umber

Raw Sienna

Sap Green

Titanium White

Other Supplies

Blending Gel Medium for Acrylic
   Paints

Soft, Lint-Free Cloth

I always feel honored when I get a glimpse of these tiny treasures, as if they have invited me to enter their special world for a few minutes. This canvas journal is a great surface for painting, and makes a wonderful gift.

PREPARATION

Prepare the Surface:

Prepare the canvas, following the instructions in the "Surfaces" section of the "Supplies" chapter.

Basecoat the Surface:

1. Mix Warm White acrylic: Titanium White acrylic + a touch of Raw Sienna acrylic. Basecoat the entire cover, using the wash brush. Let dry.
2. Place Burnt Umber acrylic and Sap Green acrylic on your dry palette. Using a palette knife, mix each color with blending gel.
3. Pick up the colors with the cloth and gently rub onto the surface, staining the lower left corner of the journal. Use more Sap Green than Burnt Umber.
4. Using a clean section of the cloth, gently rub the colors into the surface, blending as far toward the top and right side as desired. If you feel you have too much of one color, wipe away the unwanted color with a clean cloth dipped in water.
5. Let the journal cover dry for 24 hours.
6. Trace and lightly transfer the design.

Prepare to Paint the Design:

Premix the following oil color value with a palette knife:

- Light Pink: Titanium White + a touch Raw Sienna + a touch of Alizarin Crimson

PAINT THE HUMMINGBIRD

See the Ruby-Throated Hummingbird Painting Worksheet.

Eye:

1. Mix equal parts Burnt Umber + Titanium White, and thin to an inky consistency. Using the liner, paint a line around the pupil. Pull the eye ring out to form a thin triangle at each end of the eye.
2. Paint the pupil with the liner and thinned Ivory Black. Push the paint into the eye ring, narrowing it or rounding it out if necessary. Let dry.
3. Dot the highlight in the upper left area of the pupil with the liner and Titanium White.

Beak:

1. Basecoat the beak with the liner and slightly thinned Ivory Black.
2. Wipe the brush. Highlight down the center of the beak with a thin line of Titanium White.

Continued on page 72

Ruby-Throated Hummingbird Painting Worksheet

1
Basecoat.

Sap Green

Raw Umber +
Titanium White

Ivory
Black

Titanium
White

Alizarin
Crimson

2
Apply Highlights.
Add Shadows.

Yelllow Light +
Titanium White

Ivory
Black

3
Blend with the chisel edge of
the brush.

Apply scalloped
markings.

4
Deepen Shading.
Brighten Highlights.

5
Detail.

70

Columbine Painting Worksheet

1
Basecoat.

Light Pink
value

Alizarin
Crimson

Sap Green

2
Apply Shading.

Alizarin
Crimson +
Ivory Blk

Alizarin Crimson

Ivory Black

3
Blend Shading.
Apply Highlights.

Titanium
White

4
Blend Highlights.
Detail with the liner.

Cadmium
Yellow Light

Continued from page 68

Wings & Tail:

1. Mix Raw Umber + a touch of Titanium White. Basecoat the wings.
2. Shade under each feather with Raw Umber, using the chisel edge of the brush.
3. For more contrast, add a thin line of Ivory Black under each feather with the liner.
4. Add feather lines on the lower side of each feather using a liner brush.
5. Line the outside edge of each feather with the liner and thinned Titanium White.

Back & Breast:

1. Basecoat the back with Sap Green.
2. Wipe the brush. Basecoat the breast with Titanium White. Wipe the brush and chisel-blend.
3. Shade with a touch of Raw Umber near the wing and on the lower side of the belly. Wipe the brush and chisel-blend.

Head:

1. Basecoat the upper portion of the head above the eye with Sap Green.
2. While the green is wet, pick up Cadmium Yellow Light and highlight the crown. Wipe the brush and chisel-blend.
3. Using the liner and thinned Cadmium Yellow Light, add small detail lines on the crown of the head.
4. Mix equal parts Cadmium Yellow Light + Titanium White. Stipple a brighter highlight on the crown of the head with the liner.
5. Using the liner, shade below the eye with a thin line of Ivory Black.

Throat:

1. Basecoat the throat with Alizarin Crimson.
2. Mix equal parts Titanium White + Alizarin Crimson. Thin the mixture slightly and apply light scalloped markings on the throat with a liner. Make the markings smaller and increasingly faint as you move toward the beak.

Feet:

1. Add a few thin, tiny lines to indicate toes with the liner and thinned Ivory Black.

PAINT THE COLUMBINE

See the Columbine Painting Worksheet.

Cream Petals:

1. Basecoat the light petals with the Light Pink value.
2. Shade with Alizarin Crimson. Wipe the brush and pat-blend.
3. Deepen the shading with Alizarin Crimson.
4. Wipe the brush. Streak the color into the petals using the chisel edge of the brush, allowing some striations.
5. Wipe the brush. Highlight with Titanium White and pat-blend.

Red Petals:

1. Basecoat the red areas with Alizarin Crimson.
2. Shade with Alizarin Crimson + a touch of Ivory Black. Pat-blend.
3. Deepen the shading with Ivory Black. Pat-blend.
4. Add highlights with Titanium White. Wipe the brush and pat-blend.

5. Add the brightest highlights with the liner and thinned Titanium White.

Stamens:

1. Paint the stamens with the liner and thinned Titanium White.
2. Load the liner heavily with Cadmium Yellow Light. Add dots at the ends of the stamens.
3. Highlight some of the yellow dots with thicker dabs of Titanium White.

Stem:

1. Basecoat the stem with Sap Green. Let the brush run out of paint toward the bottom, so the stem fades into the background.
2. Shade with Ivory Black near the flower. Pat-blend.
3. Add the highlight near the middle of the stem with the liner and Cadmium Yellow Light. Pat-blend.

FINISHING

1. Let the painting dry for at least ten days.
2. Apply five to ten coats of spray varnish, drying to the touch after each coat.

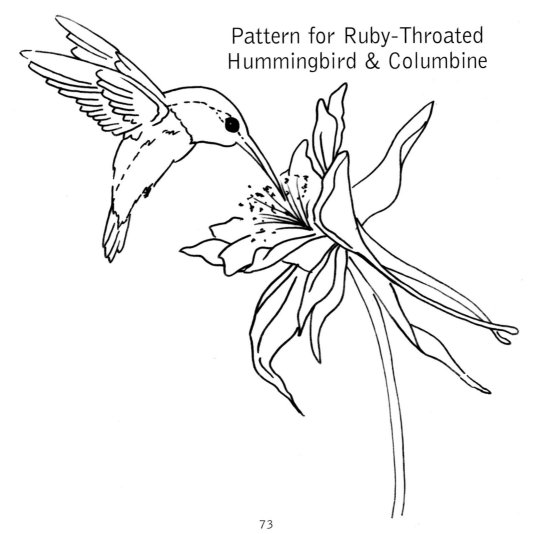

Pattern for Ruby-Throated Hummingbird & Columbine

Exotic Duo

SUPPLIES

Painting Surfaces

Two Masonite panels, 7" x 15"

Oil Palette

Alizarin Crimson

Burnt Sienna

Burnt Umber

Cadmium Yellow Light

Cobalt Blue

Cobalt Turquoise

Ivory Black

Payne's Gray

Prussian Blue

Sap Green

Titanium White

Ultramarine Blue

Brushes

Bright – #4, #6, #8

Flat Shader – #2, #10, #12

Short Liner – 10/0

Wash – ¾"

Acrylic Background Colors

Ivory Black

Sap Green

Yellow Light

The blue hyacinth macaw is one of the largest birds in the parrot family. Its feathers are rich cobalt blue, with two soft yellow areas on the face for contrast. The green conure is much smaller, with a squat body and shorter tail. Each bird is almost monochromatic, but their colors complement each other dramatically when they are framed and displayed side by side. Both parrots are lots of fun to paint!

PREPARATION

Basecoat the Surface:

1. Basecoat with the wash brush and Sap Green acrylic. Let dry.
2. Apply a second coat of Sap Green acrylic.
3. While wet, pick up a touch of Ivory Black acrylic and slip-slap it into the Sap Green.
4. Wipe the brush. Pick up Yellow Light acrylic and slip-slap it into the wet paint.
5. Continue working the acrylic colors together to achieve a mottled green. Do not overwork. Let dry.
6. Trace and transfer the pattern.

PAINT THE BACKGROUND STEMS

Follow these instructions to paint both panels.

Color Mix:

Premix the following oil color value with a palette knife:

• Violet: equal parts Ultramarine Blue + Alizarin Crimson + Titanium White

Leaf:

1. Mix equal parts Cadmium Yellow Light + Ivory Black + Sap Green to make a mid-value green. Basecoat the leaf. As you paint over the transferred lines, use the stylus to redraw the lines into the paint so you can see where to place the shading and highlights.
2. Shade with Ivory Black near the main leaf vein and on each side of the descending vein lines. Wipe the brush and pat-blend.
3. With Cadmium Yellow Light, add highlights to the center of each leaf segment and around some of the leaf edges. Wipe the brush and pat-blend the highlights.
4. Highlight each vein line with Cadmium Yellow Light, using the chisel edge of the #6 bright brush.
5. Mix equal parts Ultramarine Blue + Titanium White. Accent the leaves in some areas. Wipe the brush and pat-blend.
6. Using the Violet value, accent the leaves in other areas. Wipe the brush and pat-blend.

Branch:

1. Using Burnt Umber and the chisel edge of the #6 bright brush, basecoat the branches with choppy strokes.
2. Wipe the brush. Add highlights with Titanium White. Wipe the brush and tap the highlight into the base color to soften.
3. Wipe the brush. Accent with touches of Burnt Sienna and Violet value.

Continued on page 76

Continued from page 74

Background:

1. Mix equal parts Prussian Blue + Ivory Black. Basecoat the dark sky area with the #8 bright brush.
2. Wipe the brush. Apply a slip-slapped Titanium White highlight to indicate the moon. Wipe the brush and continue to blend and soften.

PAINT THE BLUE HYACINTH MACAW

Color Mixes:

Premix the following oil color values with a palette knife:

- Medium Blue: equal parts Cobalt Blue + Ultramarine Blue
- Dark Blue: equal parts Medium Blue + Prussian Blue
- Blue Shade: 2 parts Dark Blue + 1 part Payne's Gray
- Light Blue: Cobalt Blue + a touch of Cobalt Turquoise
- Blue Highlight: equal parts Cobalt Blue + Titanium White
- Violet: equal parts Ultramarine Blue + Alizarin Crimson + Titanium White

Eye & Base of Beak:

See the Blue Hyacinth Macaw Painting Worksheet.

1. Basecoat the ring around the eye and the yellow area at the base of the beak with the liner and a thinned mixture of Cadmium Yellow Light + a touch of Titanium White.
2. Add Burnt Sienna to the mix. Use the liner to apply dark lines to indicate wrinkles.
3. Use the liner and Titanium White to highlight around some of the wrinkles.
4. Basecoat the pupil and the nostril with the liner and Ivory Black thinned to an inky consistency.
5. Use the liner and Titanium White to highlight the pupil with a dot on the left and a comma stroke following it.
6. Using the liner and Violet value, accent the pupil with a comma stroke on the lower left curve.

Beak:

See the Blue Hyacinth Macaw Painting Worksheet.

1. Basecoat the beak with Ivory Black.
2. Using Titanium White, highlight the top curve of the upper beak and the bottom curve of the lower beak with a line starting out thick, and thinning as it curves toward the point of the beak. Pat-blend into the black.
3. Using the liner and thinned Titanium White, outline the beak with an uneven line, allowing the brush to miss some areas.
4. Using the liner, accent the beak with touches of Violet value and a mixture of Light Blue value. Blend to soften the accents; they shouldn't be overwhelming.
5. Use the liner and Titanium White to add a strong highlight with a few dots on the highlighted area of the beak.

Head:

See the Blue Hyacinth Macaw Painting Worksheet.

1. Basecoat the head and the area around the eye with the #4 bright brush and the Medium Blue value.
2. Apply the Dark Blue value mix above the eye and around the beak. Wipe the brush and chisel-blend.
3. Shade behind the eye and under the beak with the Blue Shade value. Wipe the brush and chisel-blend.

4. Apply the Light Blue value on the cheek and the top of the head. Wipe the brush and chisel-blend.
5. Use the liner and the Blue Highlight value to add touches of highlight in the brightest areas. Allow the brush to run out of color as you apply it, creating variation in value.
6. Accent with the liner and the Violet value.

Distinct Breast Feathers:

See the Exotic Duo Painting Worksheet.

1. Basecoat the breast with the Medium Blue value. As you paint over the transferred lines, use the stylus to draw the edges of the feathers so you can see where to place the shading and highlights.
2. Apply Light Blue value with the #2 flat brush. Wipe the brush and use the chisel edge to streak upward.
3. Shade under each feather with the #2 flat shader and the Blue Shade value. Wipe the brush and use the chisel edge to work the shading downward.
4. Apply Light Blue value with the liner. Begin at the tip of the feather and work the light value toward the center of the feather.
5. Wipe the liner. Apply Blue Highlight value to each feather.
6. Using the liner and Violet value, heavily accent the upper feathers and the feathers on the left side of the breast.

Wing & Tail Feathers:

1. Basecoat with Medium Blue value. As you paint over the transferred lines, use the stylus to draw the edges of the feathers so you can see where to place the shading and highlights.
2. Shade under each feather with the #2 flat brush and the Dark Blue value. Wipe the brush and use the chisel edge to work the shading downward.
3. Deepen the shading in the darkest areas with the #2 flat brush and the Blue Shade value; wipe the brush and use the chisel edge to work the shading downward.
4. Using the liner and the Light Blue value, begin at the tip of each feather and work the light value toward the center of the feather.
5. Highlight with the liner and the Blue Highlight value.
6. Accent with the liner and Violet value.

Toes:

See the Exotic Duo Painting Worksheet.

1. Basecoat the toes with the liner and Ivory Black.
2. Apply highlights down the center of each toe with the liner and Titanium White. Wipe the brush and stipple-blend to soften.
3. Accent with the Violet mix.
4. Brighten the highlights with the liner and Titanium White.

PAINT THE GREEN CONURE

Color Mixes:

Premix the following oil color values with a palette knife:

- Medium Green: equal parts Sap Green + Cadmium Yellow Light

Continued on page 79

Exotic Duo Painting Worksheet

Green Conure Wing Feathers

1 Basecoat. Apply the feather lines.

2 Streak the feather lines toward the shaft.

3 Apply shading.

4 Streak the shading outward from the shaft.

Medium Green

Light Green value feather lines.

Chisel edge of brush.

Ivory Black

Reapply the feather lines if necessary.

Streak the highlight color toward the center shaft.

Blue Hyacinth Macaw Breast Feathers

tylus nes.

1 Basecoat with Medium Blue value.

2 Apply Light Blue value.

3 Chisel-blend.

4 Apply Blue Shade value.

5 Chisel-blend. Streak the shading toward the outer edges of the feathers.

6 Detail with the liner.

Violet value accents.

Blue Highlight value

Toes

1 Basecoat.

Ivory Black

2 Apply Titanium White highlights. Stipple-blend.

3 Detail with the liner.

Highlight Titanium White.

Ivory Black segment lines.

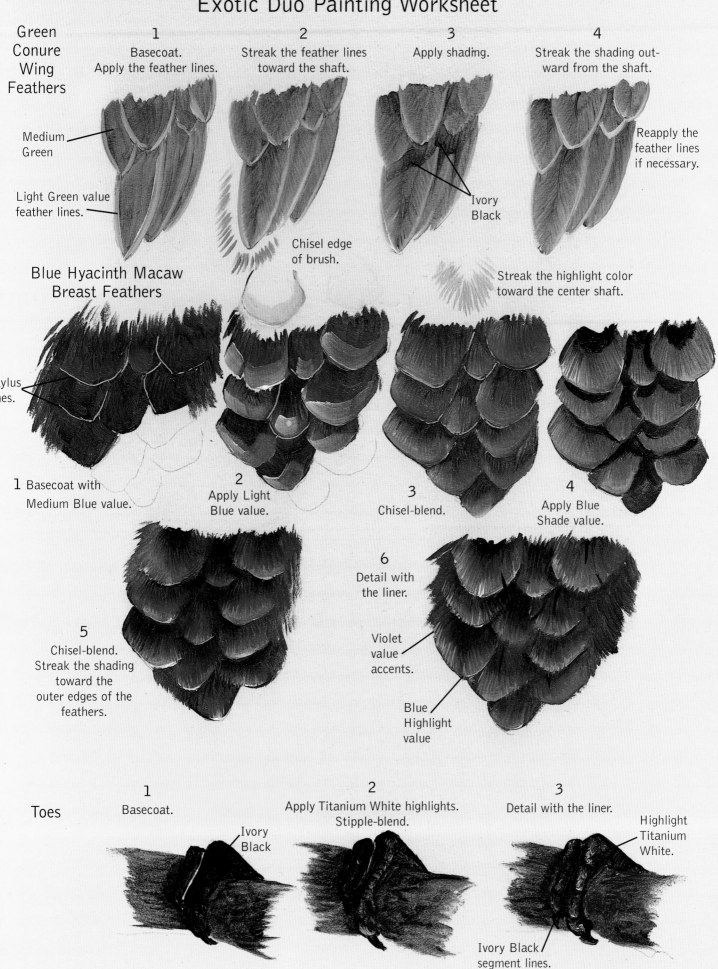

77

Blue Hyacinth Macaw Painting Worksheet

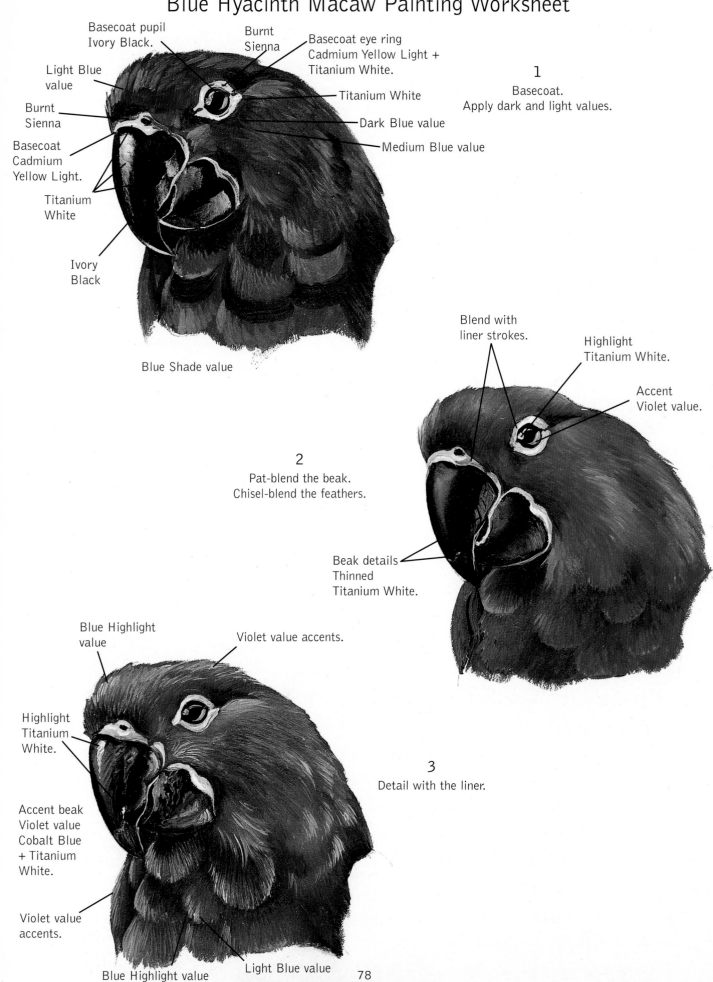

Basecoat pupil Ivory Black.

Burnt Sienna

Basecoat eye ring Cadmium Yellow Light + Titanium White.

Light Blue value

Titanium White

Burnt Sienna

Dark Blue value

Basecoat Cadmium Yellow Light.

Medium Blue value

Titanium White

Ivory Black

Blue Shade value

1
Basecoat.
Apply dark and light values.

Blend with liner strokes.

Highlight Titanium White.

Accent Violet value.

2
Pat-blend the beak.
Chisel-blend the feathers.

Beak details
Thinned Titanium White.

Blue Highlight value

Violet value accents.

Highlight Titanium White.

3
Detail with the liner.

Accent beak Violet value Cobalt Blue + Titanium White.

Violet value accents.

Blue Highlight value

Light Blue value

78

Continued from page 76

- Dark Green: equal parts Medium Green + Ivory Black
- Light Green: 1 part Medium Green + 1 part Cadmium Yellow Light + a touch of Titanium White
- Violet: equal parts Ultramarine Blue + Alizarin Crimson + Titanium White
- Medium Blue: equal parts Cobalt Blue + Ultramarine Blue
- Dark Blue: equal parts Medium Blue + Prussian Blue
- Blue Shade: 2 parts Dark Blue + 1 part Payne's Gray
- Light Blue: Cobalt Blue + a touch of Cobalt Turquoise
- Blue Highlight: equal parts Cobalt Blue + Titanium White

Eye & Face:

1. Thin a mixture of Cadmium Yellow Light + a touch of Titanium White to an inky consistency. Use the liner to paint the iris.
2. Shade the lower half of the iris with Burnt Sienna.
3. Paint a line around the iris with the liner and thinned Ivory Black. This line should be thicker at the back of the eye.
4. Paint the pupil with the liner and thinned Ivory Black.
5. Highlight the pupil with a dot of Titanium White.
6. Basecoat the light area around the eye and the beak with Titanium White.
7. Add shading close to the bottom of the beak and around the eye with a mixture of Prussian Blue + Alizarin Crimson. Blend into the Titanium White.
8. Using the liner and thinned Ivory Black, paint the nostril. Paint lines around the eye. Make them uneven and slightly squiggly to suggest wrinkles.
9. Highlight around some of the wrinkles, and the lower curve of the nostril, with the liner and touches of Titanium White.

Beak:

1. Basecoat the beak with Ivory Black.
2. Using Titanium White, highlight the top curve of the upper beak and the bottom curve of the lower beak with a line starting out thick, and thinning as it curves toward the point of the beak. Pat-blend into the black.
3. Using the liner and thinned Titanium White, outline the beak with an uneven line, allowing the brush to miss some areas.
4. Using the liner, accent the beak with touches of the Violet value and a mix of Cobalt Blue + a touch of Titanium White. Blend to soften the accents; they shouldn't be overwhelming.
5. Use the liner and Titanium White to add a strong highlight with a few dots in the highlighted area on the beak.

Head, Breast & Shoulder:

1. Basecoat the head, breast, and shoulder with the #4 bright brush and the Medium Green value.
2. Apply Ivory Black shading below the beak, above the nostril area, and around the white area of the head. Wipe the brush and chisel-blend.
3. Apply the Light Green value on the cheek, the top of the head, and the throat. Wipe the brush and chisel-blend.

Continued on next page

Continued from page 79

4. Add touches of highlight in the brightest areas of the head with the liner and Titanium White. Allow the brush to run out of color as you apply, creating variations in value. Continue to lighten the crown of the head to create contrast.
5. Shade the breast with Dark Green value near the wing feathers. Wipe the brush and chisel blend.
6. Highlight the outer area of the breast with the Light Green value.
7. Accent with the liner and the Violet value.

Green Wing & Tail Feathers:
See the Exotic Duo Painting Worksheet.
1. Basecoat with the Medium Green value. As you paint over the transferred lines, use the stylus to draw the edge of the feather so you can see where to place the shading and highlights.
2. Apply the feather line using the chisel edge of the #2 flat brush and the Light Green value. Wipe the brush and streak lines toward the center of the feather with the chisel edge.
3. Shade under each feather with the #2 flat brush and Ivory Black. Wipe the brush and use the chisel edge to work the shading down and out toward the feather edges.
4. Highlight each feather with the liner and Titanium White.
5. Accent the feathers with the liner and Violet value.

Blue Wing & Tail Feathers:
1. Basecoat with the Medium Blue value. As you paint over the transferred lines, use the stylus to draw the edges of the feathers so you can see where to place the shading and highlights.
2. Shade under each feather with the #2 flat brush and the Dark Blue value. Wipe the brush and use the chisel edge to work the shading downward.
3. Deepen the shading in the darkest areas with the #2 flat brush and the Blue Shade value. Wipe the brush and use the chisel edge to work the shading downward.
4. Using the liner and the Light Blue value, begin at the tip of each feather and work the light value toward the center of the feather.
5. Highlight with the liner and the Blue Highlight value.
6. Accent with the liner and Violet value.

Toes:
See the Exotic Duo Painting Worksheet.
1. Basecoat the toes with the liner and Ivory Black.
2. Apply highlights down the center of each toe with the liner and Titanium White. Wipe the brush and stipple-blend to soften.
3. Paint segment lines with the liner and Ivory Black.
4. Brighten the highlights with the liner and Titanium White.

FINISHING

1. Let the painting dry for at least ten days.
2. Apply five to ten coats of spray varnish, drying to the touch after each coat.

Pattern for Green Conure
Enlarge @200% for actual size.

Pattern for Blue Hyacinth Macaw
Enlarge @200% for actual size.

Blue Jay

SUPPLIES

Painting Surface
Masonite panel, 8" x 10"

Oil Palette
Alizarin Crimson
Burnt Sienna
Burnt Umber
Cadmium Yellow Light
Cerulean Blue
Ivory Black
Payne's Gray
Prussian Blue
Raw Sienna
Titanium White
Ultramarine Blue
Yellow Ochre

Brushes
Bright – #4, #8
Flat Shader – #2, #10, #12
Short Liner – 10/0
Wash – ¾"

Acrylic Background Colors
Basil Green premixed craft acrylic
Dove Gray premixed craft acrylic
Titanium White

Other Supplies
High-Density Foam Roller, 4"
Toothbrush for spattering

They awaken my little girl and me with their loud calls, and we excitedly await a glimpse of these vivid blue birds. They nest in our yard, so we can enjoy them daily, summer or winter. Their blue feathers are even brighter in a snowy landscape.

PREPARATION

Apply the Multicolored Eggshell Finish:
1. Basecoat with Dove Gray acrylic, using the foam roller.
2. While wet, drizzle on Basil Green acrylic, Titanium White acrylic, and more Dove Gray acrylic. While the paint is wet, blend the colors with the roller. Let dry.

Prepare to Paint the Design:
1. Trace and transfer the design.
2. Premix the following oil color mix with a palette knife:
   Gray Blue: 1 part Ultramarine Blue + 1 part Cerulean Blue + 1 part Titanium White + a touch of Payne's Gray + a touch of Alizarin Crimson

PAINT THE BLUE JAY

See the Blue Jay Painting Worksheet.
Eye:
1. Basecoat the iris with the liner and Burnt Sienna.
2. Highlight the lower curve of the iris with a curved stroke, using the liner and slightly thinned Raw Sienna.
3. Basecoat the eye ring with the liner and Ivory Black.
4. Paint the pupil with the liner and thinned Ivory Black.
5. Use the liner to highlight the pupil and iris with a small, elongated dot of Titanium White.

Head:
1. Basecoat the black areas with the liner and Ivory Black.
2. Basecoat the crown, back of the neck, and shoulder with the Gray Blue mix.
3. Basecoat above the beak with the liner and Gray Blue mix.
4. Highlight with Titanium White. Wipe the brush and chisel-blend.
5. Shade with Prussian Blue. Wipe the brush and chisel-blend.
6. Basecoat the white areas above and below the eye with Titanium White + a touch of Gray Blue mix.
7. Shade the white areas with the liner and the Gray Blue mix.
8. Mix equal parts Alizarin Crimson + Titanium White. Accent the Gray Blue mix area near the front of the shoulder and where desired with a touch of the mixture. Wipe the brush and chisel-blend.
9. Accent the throat, the back of the head, and the shoulder with Yellow Ochre. Wipe the brush and chisel-blend.

Continued on page 84

Continued from page 82

Beak:

1. Basecoat the beak with the liner and Ivory Black.
2. Use the liner and Titanium White to highlight above and below the line where the upper and lower beak meet, and the tip of the beak. Wipe the brush and blend with small liner strokes.
3. Paint a small dot for the nostril with the liner and Ivory Black.

Wings & Tail Feathers:

1. Basecoat the smaller covert feathers with the Gray Blue mix.
2. Highlight the outer edge of each feather with a small feather line of Titanium White.
3. Basecoat the long primary flying feathers and the tail with the Gray Blue mix + a touch more Ultramarine Blue. Leave a small, unpainted triangle on the end of each primary wing feather. As you paint over the transferred lines, use the stylus to draw the edge of the feather so you can see where to place the shading and highlights.
4. Basecoat the small white triangles on the wing feathers with the liner and slightly thinned Titanium White. Pull a stroke up with the chisel edge of the brush to highlight the outer edges of the feathers.
5. Shade the tail at the base and where one feather overlaps another with Payne's Gray. Wipe the brush and chisel-blend.
6. Highlight the tips of the long wing primaries and the tail feathers. Wipe the brush and chisel-blend the highlight into the primaries, pulling strokes up. Using the chisel edge of the brush, pull strokes toward the center shaft of the tail feathers.
7. Using the chisel edge of the brush and Titanium White, pull strokes up to highlight the edges of the tail feathers.
8. Use the liner and thinned Ivory Black to paint the black markings on the primary feathers and tail.

Breast:

1. Basecoat with Titanium White.
2. Shade lightly near the wings with a touch of the Gray Blue mix. Wipe the brush and chisel blend.

Toes:

1. Basecoat the toes with the liner and Ivory Black.
2. Apply highlights down the center of each toe with the liner and Titanium White. Wipe the brush and gently tap to soften.
3. Paint segment lines with the liner and Ivory Black.
4. Highlight again if needed.

PAINT THE BRANCHES

Branches:

See the Blue Jay Painting Worksheet.

1. Mix 1 part Burnt Umber + 1 part Ultramarine Blue + a touch of Titanium White. Basecoat the branch with the #4 bright brush. Wipe the brush.
2. Accent the branch with a small amount of Burnt Sienna.
3. Pick up globs of Titanium White with the liner and paint irregular clumps of snow on the top surface of the branch.
4. Thin the Burnt Umber mixture from Step 1 to wash consistency. Paint the background tree branches with the #4 bright brush.
5. Thin Titanium White to wash consistency and add some soft snow with the liner to the closer background branch.

FINISHING

1. Use an old toothbrush to spatter thinned Titanium White on painting.
2. Let the painting dry for at least ten days.
3. Apply five to ten coats of spray varnish, drying to the touch after each coat.

Pattern for Blue Jay

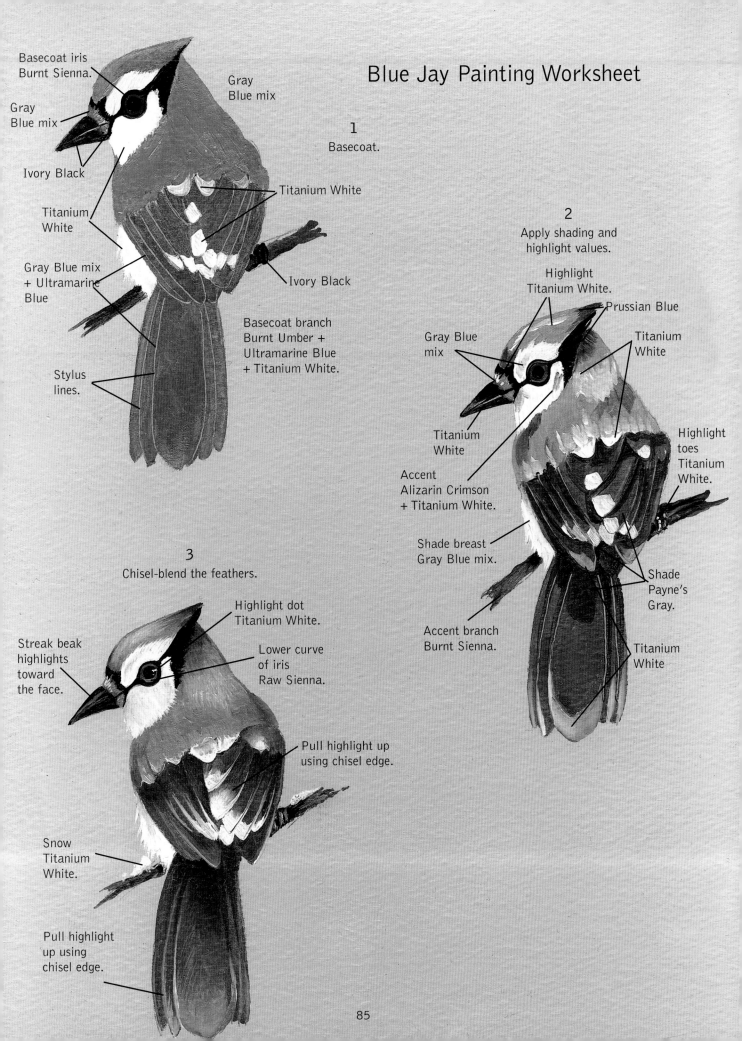

Blue Jay Painting Worksheet

1
Basecoat.

Basecoat iris
Burnt Sienna.

Gray
Blue mix

Gray
Blue mix

Ivory Black

Titanium White

Titanium
White

Titanium White

Ivory Black

Gray Blue mix
+ Ultramarine
Blue

Basecoat branch
Burnt Umber +
Ultramarine Blue
+ Titanium White.

Stylus
lines.

2
Apply shading and
highlight values.

Highlight
Titanium White.

Prussian Blue

Gray Blue
mix

Titanium
White

Titanium
White

Highlight
toes
Titanium
White.

Accent
Alizarin Crimson
+ Titanium White.

Shade breast
Gray Blue mix.

Shade
Payne's
Gray.

Accent branch
Burnt Sienna.

Titanium
White

3
Chisel-blend the feathers.

Highlight dot
Titanium White.

Lower curve
of iris
Raw Sienna.

Streak beak
highlights
toward
the face.

Pull highlight up
using chisel edge.

Snow
Titanium
White.

Pull highlight
up using
chisel edge.

85

Baby Bunny & Magnolias

I have long been a fan of all the critters that stick around in the winter. There's nothing better than seeing a familiar face when it's -35 degrees outside.

SUPPLIES

Painting Surface

Plaque, 11" x 11" with 6" x 9" oval center

Oil Palette

Burnt Sienna

Burnt Umber

Cadmium Red Medium

Cadmium Yellow Light

Ivory Black

Raw Sienna

Titanium White

Ultramarine Blue

Yellow Ochre

Brushes

Bright – #4, #8

Flat Shader – #2, #10, #12

Grainer – ⅜"

Short Liner – 10/0

Wash – ¾"

Acrylic Background Colors

Raw Sienna

Sap Green

Titanium White

Other Supplies

High-Density Foam Roller, 4"

Toothbrush for spattering

PREPARATION

Prepare the Surface:

Prepare the surface, following the instructions in the "Surfaces" section of the "Supplies" chapter.

Apply the Multicolored Eggshell Finish Background:

1. Mix Warm White acrylic: Titanium White acrylic + a touch of Raw Sienna acrylic. Basecoat the plaque, using the foam roller. Let dry.
2. Basecoat the oval area again with the Warm White acrylic mix.
3. While wet, drizzle on a touch of Titanium White acrylic and a touch of Raw Sienna acrylic on the oval area. Blend the wet acrylics with the roller. Let dry.
4. Mix Sap Green acrylic with Titanium White acrylic to get a light green. Thin with water and use to paint the raised trim around the oval and the edge of the plaque. Let dry.
5. Using Warm White acrylic mix, paint the trim and the incised leaf design. This makes a slight difference in background colors and cleans up the edges.
6. Trace and transfer the design.

PAINT THE BUNNY

See the Bunny Painting Worksheet.

Eye:

1. Paint the ring around the eye with the liner and Burnt Sienna.
2. Basecoat the pupil with the liner and Ivory Black.
3. Use the liner to highlight the pupil with a stroke of Titanium White on the lower left curve of the eye. Place one large dot in the upper center and two small dots on the upper right curve.
4. Use the liner and Titanium White to add little dots on the eye ring to highlight.

Ears:

1. Mix equal parts Burnt Sienna + Titanium White + Raw Sienna. Basecoat the far ear.
2. Shade the far ear with Raw Sienna, then Burnt Sienna. Wipe the brush and pat-blend to merge and soften the values.

Continued on page 88

Continued from page 86

3. Mix Titanium White + a touch of Raw Sienna. Basecoat the foreground ear.

4. Accent the inner ear at the top with the mixture from Step 1. Wipe the brush and pat-blend.

5. Highlight the foreground ear with Titanium White. Wipe the brush and pat-blend.

6. Mix equal parts Cadmium Red Medium + Titanium White. Accent the inner ear. Wipe the brush and pat-blend.

7. Mix Burnt Umber + a touch of Ivory Black. Accent the far ear. Wipe the brush and pat-blend.

8. Thin Titanium White to a wash consistency. Paint very soft, tiny veins in the ear with the liner.

9. Paint the thin line around the foreground ear with the liner and Titanium White.

Fur, Step 1 – Basecoat:

Use the chisel edge of the bright brushes to apply the values.

1. Mix Titanium White + a touch of Raw Sienna. Basecoat around the eye, the light area under the nose, and the top of the nose.

2. Apply Burnt Umber behind the cheek, around the white near the eye, and where the bunny is tucked behind the flowers. Apply in front of the ear and at the top of the forehead.

3. Apply a line of Burnt Umber in the nostril area of the nose.

4. Mix a medium value with Raw Sienna + a touch of Burnt Umber. Basecoat the rest of the fur.

5. Highlight the neck behind the ears, the very top of the nose, and in front of the dark area of the cheek with Titanium White.

Fur, Step 2 – Blend:

Blend with the chisel edge of the brush, following the growth direction. Wipe the brush as needed. Remember that the fur strokes are shorter near the nose and around the eye and lengthen as you move away from the face.

Fur, Step 3 – Overstroke:

1. Mix 1 part Raw Sienna + 1 part Titanium White + a touch of Burnt Umber. Thin to a light brown-gray value and begin to overlay the fur with liner strokes. Reload the brush frequently. As you stroke over the fur, let the brush run out of paint to create variations in the values.

2. Mix equal parts Raw Sienna + Titanium White. Highlight with liner strokes.

PAINT THE MAGNOLIAS

Petals:

See the Magnolia Painting Worksheet.

1. Mix Titanium White + a touch of Raw Sienna. Basecoat the petals.

2. Mix equal parts Yellow Ochre + Raw Sienna. Shade each petal near the flower center, under the flips, and where one petal overlaps another. Wipe the brush and pat-blend to merge and soften the values.

3. Shade the very darkest areas with a bit of Burnt Sienna. Wipe the brush and pat-blend.

4. Highlight each petal with Titanium White. Wipe the brush and pat-blend.

5. Highlight the petal flips with the liner and Titanium White.

Flower Centers:

See the Magnolia Painting Worksheet.

1. Mix equal parts Yellow Ochre + Titanium White. Basecoat the centers.

2. Mix equal parts Raw Sienna + Burnt Sienna. Shade the centers. Wipe the brush and pat-blend.

3. Mix equal parts Burnt Umber + Burnt Sienna. Use the liner to stipple dots on the lower part of the center.

4. Stipple the highlight with the liner and Cadmium Yellow Light.

5. Stipple the brightest highlights with the liner and Titanium White.

Leaves:

1. Premix the following oil color values with a palette knife:
   • Medium Green: 5 parts Cadmium Yellow Light + 1 part Ivory Black + a touch of Titanium White
   • Dark Green: Medium Green + a touch of Ivory Black
   • Light Green: equal parts Medium Green + Cadmium Yellow Light

2. Using the Dark Green value, basecoat above the curve of the vein line, at the base of the leaf, and where one leaf overlaps another.

3. Basecoat the rest of the leaf with the Medium Green value. Wipe the brush and pat-blend.

4. Apply the Light Green value under the vein line. Wipe the brush and pat-blend.

5. Continue to apply and blend the values until you achieve the desired contrast.

6. Stipple the brightest leaf highlights with the liner and Titanium White.

7. Mix equal parts Ultramarine Blue + Titanium White. Apply accents to several leaves of your choice. Pat-blend to soften the accents into the leaves.

8. Apply Raw Sienna accents to other leaves. Pat-blend to soften.

9. Thin some of the blue mixture. Using the liner, add a thin line to provide contrast where one leaf overlaps another.

FINISHING

1. Thin Raw Sienna acrylic paint to the consistency of ink. Dip the bristles of an old toothbrush into the thinned paint. With the bristles pointed down, pull your thumb or the edge of a palette knife across the bristles, pulling toward your body to release a spray of fine dots across the surface. You may wish to practice on scrap paper before spattering on your painting.

2. Let the painting dry for at least ten days.

3. Apply five to ten coats of spray varnish, drying to the touch after each coat.

Highlight & Shading Diagram

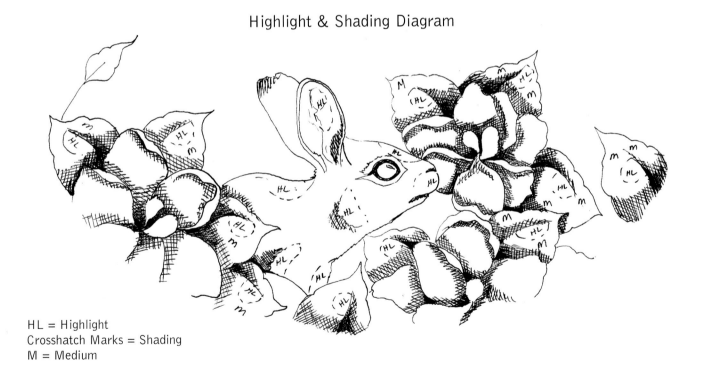

HL = Highlight
Crosshatch Marks = Shading
M = Medium

89

Bunny Painting Worksheet

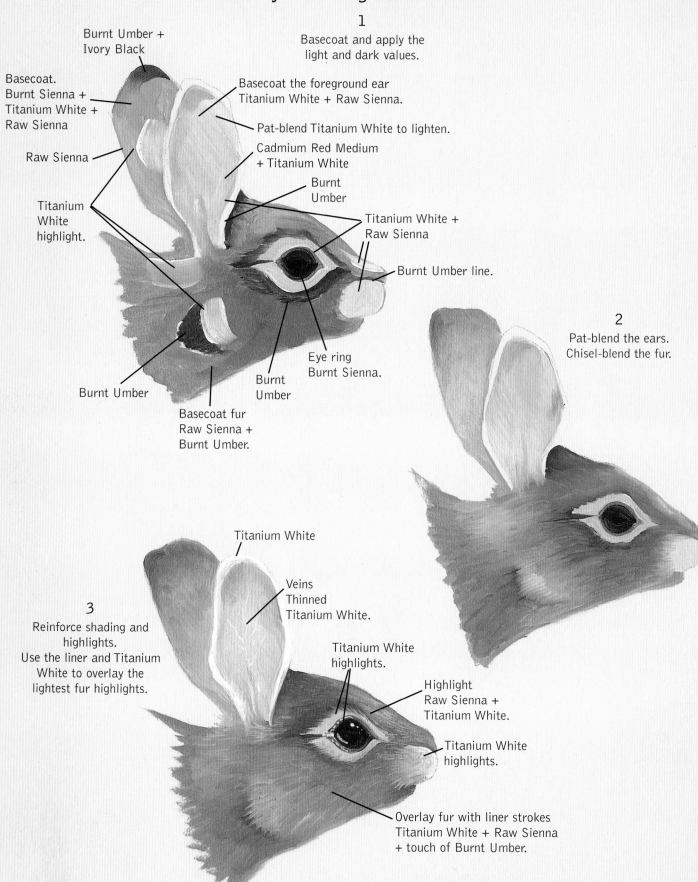

1
Basecoat and apply the
light and dark values.

Burnt Umber +
Ivory Black

Basecoat the foreground ear
Titanium White + Raw Sienna.

Basecoat.
Burnt Sienna +
Titanium White +
Raw Sienna

Pat-blend Titanium White to lighten.

Raw Sienna

Cadmium Red Medium
+ Titanium White

Burnt
Umber

Titanium
White
highlight.

Titanium White +
Raw Sienna

Burnt Umber line.

Eye ring
Burnt Sienna.

Burnt Umber

Burnt
Umber

Basecoat fur
Raw Sienna +
Burnt Umber.

2
Pat-blend the ears.
Chisel-blend the fur.

3
Reinforce shading and
highlights.
Use the liner and Titanium
White to overlay the
lightest fur highlights.

Titanium White

Veins
Thinned
Titanium White.

Titanium White
highlights.

Highlight
Raw Sienna +
Titanium White.

Titanium White
highlights.

Overlay fur with liner strokes
Titanium White + Raw Sienna
+ touch of Burnt Umber.

90

Magnolia Painting Worksheet

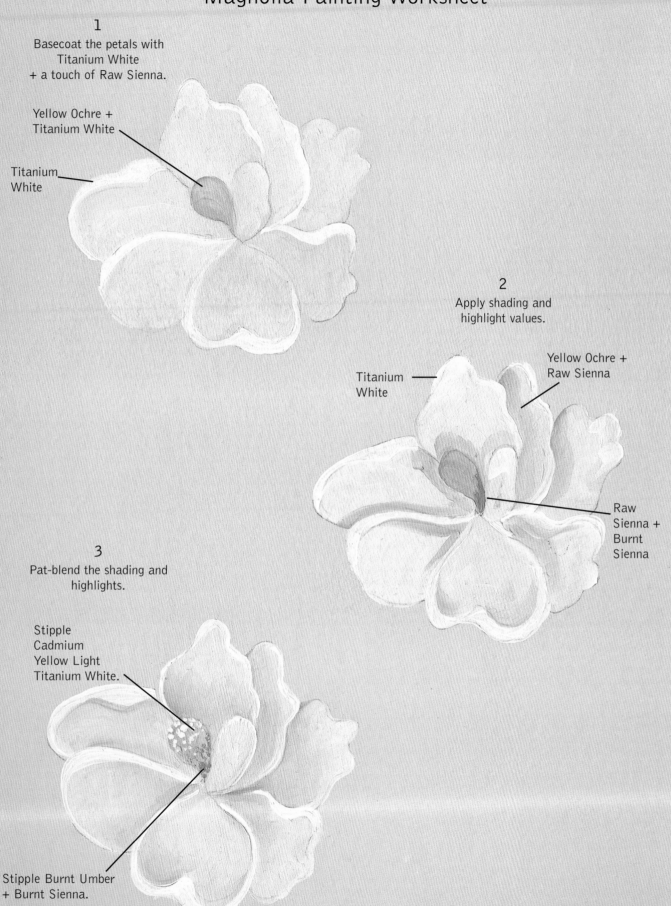

1
Basecoat the petals with
Titanium White
+ a touch of Raw Sienna.

Yellow Ochre +
Titanium White

Titanium
White

2
Apply shading and
highlight values.

Titanium
White

Yellow Ochre +
Raw Sienna

Raw
Sienna +
Burnt
Sienna

3
Pat-blend the shading and
highlights.

Stipple
Cadmium
Yellow Light
Titanium White.

Stipple Burnt Umber
+ Burnt Sienna.

Pattern for
Baby Bunny
& Magnolias

Doe in the Forest

Capture a moment of perfect serenity in this painting, as the delicate doe pauses to gaze at a butterfly fluttering into her forest clearing. The doe's expressive ears get their translucent quality from pat-blending the rosy pinks and browns of the inner ear.

SUPPLIES

Painting Surface
Canvas, 9" x 12"

Oil Palette
Burnt Sienna
Burnt Umber
Cadmium Red Medium
Cadmium Yellow Light
French Ultramarine
Ivory Black
Raw Sienna
Sap Green
Titanium White
Yellow Ochre

Brushes
Bright – #2, #4, #8
Flat Shader – #2, #10, #12
Filbert Grainer – ⅜"
Short Liner – 10/0
Wash – ¾"
Lunar Blender – ¼", ⅜"

Acrylic Background Colors
Titanium White
Raw Sienna

PREPARATION

Prepare the Surface:
Prepare the canvas, following the instructions in the "Surfaces" section of the "Supplies" chapter.

Basecoat the Surface:
1. Mix Warm White acrylic: Titanium White acrylic + touch of Raw Sienna acrylic. Basecoat the canvas, using the wash brush. Let dry.
2. Apply as many coats as needed to achieve opaque coverage, drying after each coat.
3. Trace and transfer the design.

Color Mixes:
Premix the following oil color values with a palette knife:
- Medium Brown: 1 part Raw Sienna + 1 part Yellow Ochre + a touch of Burnt Sienna
- Light Brown: equal parts Yellow Ochre + Raw Sienna
- Highlight value: equal parts Yellow Ochre + Titanium White
- Baby Pink: equal parts Cadmium Red Medium + Burnt Sienna + Titanium White

PAINT THE DOE

See the Doe Painting Worksheet.

Eyes & Nose:
To give the paint time to set, complete the painting before applying the final highlights to the eye and nose. Instructions are in the "Final Touches" section.
1. Basecoat the eye and nose with Ivory Black.
2. Using the liner and Titanium White, tap a highlight on the top of the nose and around the nostril. Wipe the liner and gently stipple-blend to soften.
3. Use a liner and a slightly thinned mixture of equal parts Ivory Black + Burnt Umber to paint the nostrils and the area between the nose and mouth.

Inner Ears:
1. Basecoat the inner center area with the Baby Pink value.
2. Basecoat the rest of the inner ear with the Medium Brown value.
3. Shade with Burnt Umber. Wipe the brush and pat-blend.

Continued on page 96

94

Continued from page 94

4. Highlight the outer rims with the Highlight value.
5. Use the liner and slightly thinned Titanium White to add the fine hairs of the inner ears.

Fur:

Use the chisel edge of the brush and always follow the growth direction.

1. Using Burnt Umber, apply the dark value just above and to the left of the nose, in front of the eye and in the eyebrow area, on the base of the outer ear, on the head near the ear, on the cheek, and on the shoulder.
2. Basecoat the underside of the face and the neck with Titanium White.
3. Basecoat the rest of the doe with the Medium Brown value.
4. Chisel-blend the values with the bright or lunar blender together to soften. Wipe the brush frequently.
5. Shade under the nose, behind the mouth, and under the jaw with the Light Brown value. Apply shading sparsely. Wipe the brush and chisel-blend.
6. Shade above the nose and in the front corner of the eyes with Burnt Umber. Apply shading sparsely. Wipe the brush and chisel-blend.
7. Highlight the area around the eyes with the Light Brown value. Wipe the brush and chisel-blend.
8. Strengthen the highlights around the eye with the Highlight value. Wipe the brush and chisel-blend.
9. Use the Light Brown value mix under the cheek and on the neck. Wipe the brush and chisel-blend.
10. Apply the Highlight value under the cheek and on the neck. Wipe the brush and chisel-blend.
11. Use the liner and the Highlight value to detail under the cheek and on the neck with some very bright highlights.
12. Referring to the photo, shade and highlight the doe's body, always using the chisel edge of the brush and following the growth direction.

Tail:

1. Using Burnt Umber and the chisel edge of the ¼" lunar blender, chop the dark value randomly on the tail.
2. Paint the rest of the tail with Medium Brown value. Wipe the brush and chisel-blend.
3. Highlight edges of the tail and a few places on the tail with the Highlight value and the #4 bright brush.

PAINT THE BUTTERFLY

1. Basecoat the wings with the #2 bright and a mixture of equal parts Cadmium Yellow Light + Titanium White.
2. Apply Medium Brown value shading on the hind wings where they are overlapped by the forewings. Wipe the brush and stipple-blend.
3. Using the liner and Titanium White, highlight with streaks through the center of each wing and on the edges.
4. Detail the butterfly wings and paint the body with the liner and thinned Burnt Umber.

PAINT THE FOREST BACKGROUND

1. Mix equal parts French Ultramarine + Sap Green. Mix equal parts Burnt Umber + Burnt Sienna. Block in the background using the slip-slap technique, overlapping layers.
2. Add touches of Yellow Ochre, Cadmium Yellow Light, or French Ultramarine + Titanium White to add interest. Apply in random, haphazard strokes.
3. Wipe the brush. Load in a brush mix of equal parts Sap Green + Cadmium Yellow Light. Use the corner of the brush to tap highlights in the foliage areas to indicate background trees and forest undergrowth. Apply some leafy highlight shapes where the legs vanish.

FINAL TOUCHES

1. Use the liner and Titanium White to apply a dot for the bright, round highlight on the eye.
2. Add the curved highlight at the top of the eye with the liner and slightly thinned Titanium White.
3. Using the liner and Titanium White, add strong highlights (glints) to the nose and the nostrils. Do not place the highlights in a solid line, but apply in a hit-and-miss fashion.
4. Using the liner and slightly thinned Ivory Black, paint the black line around the eye.
5. Use the liner and the Highlight value to highlight around the eye with fur-like strokes.

FINISHING

1. Let the painting dry for at least ten days.
2. Apply five to ten coats of spray varnish, drying to the touch after each coat.

Doe Painting Worksheet

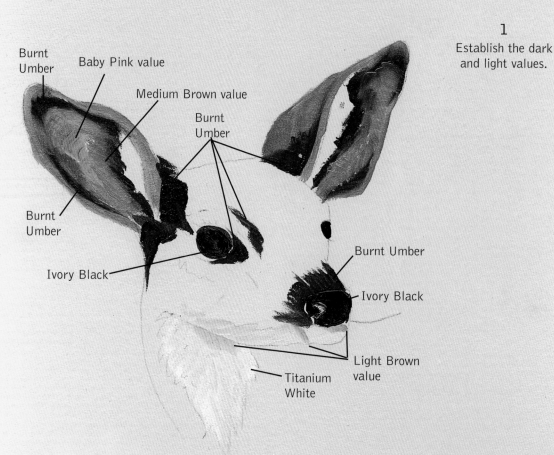

Burnt Umber

Baby Pink value

Medium Brown value

Burnt Umber

1
Establish the dark
and light values.

Burnt Umber

Ivory Black

Burnt Umber

Ivory Black

Light Brown value

Titanium White

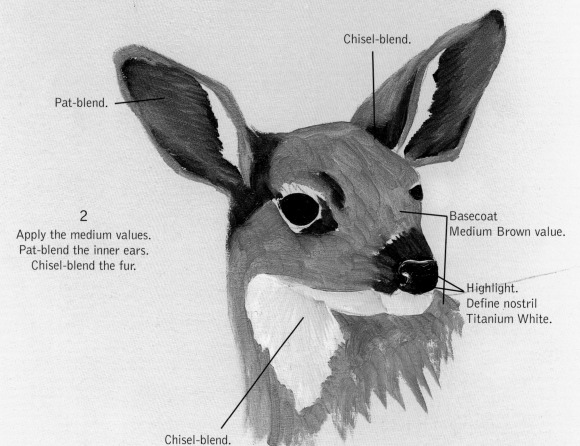

Chisel-blend.

Pat-blend.

Basecoat
Medium Brown value.

2
Apply the medium values.
Pat-blend the inner ears.
Chisel-blend the fur.

Highlight.
Define nostril
Titanium White.

Chisel-blend.

Doe Painting Worksheet

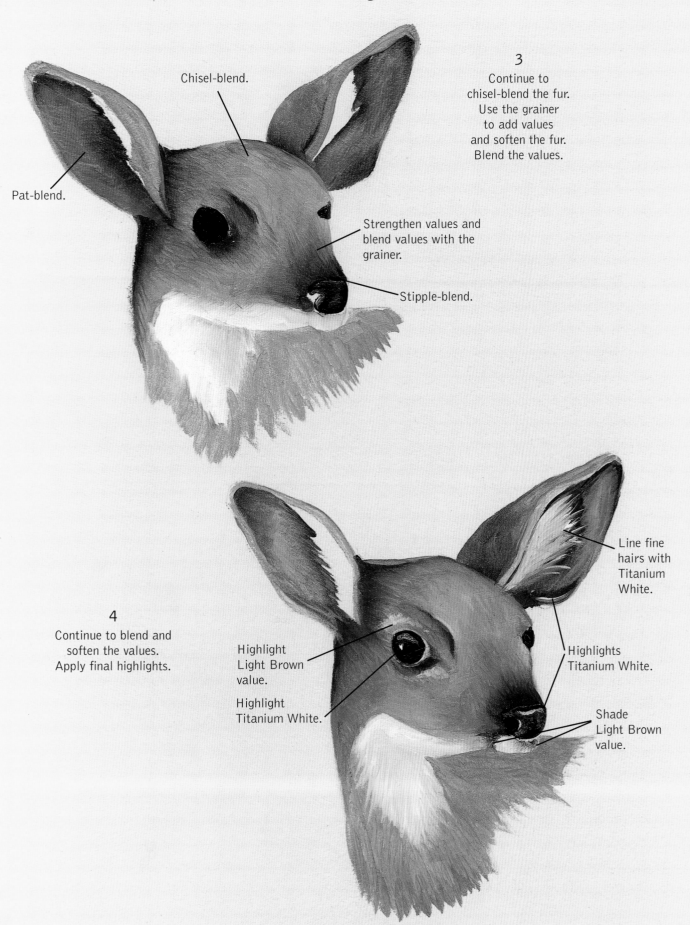

Chisel-blend.

Pat-blend.

3
Continue to
chisel-blend the fur.
Use the grainer
to add values
and soften the fur.
Blend the values.

Strengthen values and
blend values with the
grainer.

Stipple-blend.

4
Continue to blend and
soften the values.
Apply final highlights.

Highlight
Light Brown
value.

Highlight
Titanium White.

Line fine
hairs with
Titanium
White.

Highlights
Titanium White.

Shade
Light Brown
value.

Pattern for
Doe in the Forest

Pattern for Chipmunk & Fruit

Instructions begin on page 102.

Chipmunk & Fruit

Without the chipmunk, this painting would be an old-world still life, but I would miss the sneaky little guy looking for a meal. The color of the matting on this piece was a risky choice that paid off, and is an example of how great framing can make a painting more dynamic.

SUPPLIES

Painting Surface
Canvas, 10" x 10"

Oil Palette
Alizarin Crimson
Burnt Sienna
Burnt Umber
Cadmium Red Deep (Hue)
Cadmium Red Light (Hue)
Cadmium Red Medium
Cadmium Yellow Light
Ivory Black
Prussian Blue
Raw Sienna
Sap Green
Titanium White
Ultramarine Blue
Yellow Green
Yellow Ochre

Brushes
Bright – #4, #8
Flat Shader – #2, #10, #12
Grainer – ⅜"
Mop – ½"
Short Liner – 10/0
Wash – ¾"

Acrylic Background Colors
Titanium White
Raw Sienna

Other Supplies
Linseed Oil

PREPARATION

Prepare the Surface:
Prepare the canvas, following the instructions in the "Surfaces" section of the "Supplies" chapter.

Basecoat the Surface:
1. Mix Warm White acrylic: Titanium White acrylic + a touch of Raw Sienna acrylic. Basecoat the canvas, using the wash brush. Let dry.
2. Apply as many coats as needed to achieve opaque coverage, drying after each coat.
3. Trace and transfer the design.

Color Mixes:
Premix the following oil color values with a palette knife:
• Highlight Brown: equal parts Yellow Ochre + Titanium White
• Light Brown: 2 parts Yellow Ochre + 1 part Medium Brown
• Medium Brown: equal parts Raw Sienna + Burnt Sienna
• Dark Brown: equal parts Medium Brown + Burnt Umber

PAINT THE FRUIT

Apple:
See the Apple Painting Worksheet.
1. Apply Alizarin Crimson in a crescent shape on the left side of the apple.
2. Apply Cadmium Red Deep next to the shadow.
3. Apply Cadmium Red Light near the top right, below the area that will be green.
4. Pat-blend all the red areas.
5. Basecoat the green areas with Yellow Green.
6. Mix 5 parts Yellow Green + 1 part Ivory Black. Apply to the indentation for the stem.
7. Mix equal parts Titanium White + Cadmium Yellow Light. Highlight the green area.
8. With the #4 bright brush, chisel-blend where the green and red areas meet. Wipe the brush frequently so as not to drag red into the green area and vice versa.
9. Wipe the brush. Blend the green values with the chisel edge.

Continued on page 104

Continued from page 102

10. Soften the blending with the mop brush.

11. Strengthen the shadows and highlights. Wipe the brush and chisel-blend.

12. Stem: Paint the stem with the liner and a mix of Yellow Green + a touch of Ivory Black. Shade with Ivory Black and highlight with Cadmium Yellow Light. Further highlight with dots of Titanium White.

Cherries:

Refer to the Cherries Painting Worksheet in the "Chickadee & Cherries" project, but use the colors listed in the instructions below.

1. For the dark value, mix Alizarin Crimson + a touch of Ivory Black. Apply with choppy strokes to create crescent-shaped shadows on the dark sides of the cherries. Leave a line at the edge of the shadowed side of selected cherries for a reflected light. (This line will be painted with the medium value.)

2. Fill in the remainder of the cherry with Cadmium Red Deep (the medium value). Wipe the brush and choppily connect the dark and medium values.

3. Paint the reflected light lines with Cadmium Red Medium.

4. For the light value, mix Cadmium Yellow Light + a touch of Titanium White. Using the liner, stipple where the light would hit the cherry, usually opposite the crescent. Stipple-blend to soften.

5. Continue to stipple progressively brighter highlights with Cadmium Yellow Light, then Titanium White.

6. Accent the side of the cherry that overlaps another design element (in this case, the left side) with the liner and thinned Ultramarine Blue + Titanium White.

7. Stem: Paint the same as apple stems.

PAINT THE CHIPMUNK

See the Chipmunk Painting Worksheet.

Eye:

1. Paint the ring around the eye with the liner and Burnt Sienna.

2. Basecoat the pupil with the liner and Ivory Black.

3. Use the liner and Titanium White to add little dots on the eye ring to highlight.

4. Highlight the pupil with the liner and Titanium White, as shown on the Painting Worksheet.

Ears:

1. Basecoat the inner ear with the Dark Brown value.

2. Shade with the liner and a touch of Ivory Black near the bottom of the ear. Gently pat-blend to connect and soften the values.

3. Basecoat the outer ear edge with the Medium Brown value. Wipe the brush and pat-blend.

4. Highlight the outer ear edge with the liner and Light Brown value. Wipe the brush and pat-blend.

5. Add the thin line on the outer ear with the liner and Titanium White.

Fur, Step 1 – Basecoat:

Use the chisel edge of the #4 bright brush to apply the values.

1. Basecoat around the eye with the Light Brown value.

2. Basecoat the light area under the nose, on the chest, and on the edge of the cheek with the Light Brown value.

3. Using the Dark Brown value, apply the stripe from the nose to the light area around the eye, and above and below the light brown area.

4. Basecoat the dark stripes on the back with the Dark Brown value.

5. Using Titanium White, basecoat the white stripes on the back with choppy strokes.

6. Apply a little Light Brown value to shade the white back stripes near the head.

7. Basecoat the rest of the fur with the Medium Brown value.

Fur, Step 2 – Blend:

1. Blend with the chisel edge of the #4 bright, following the growth direction. Wipe the brush frequently. Remember that the fur strokes are shorter near the nose and around the eye and lengthen as you move away from the face.

2. Referring to the photo, continue to shade, highlight, and blend the chipmunk's body.

Fur, Step 3 – Overstroke:

1. Highlight the cheek, forehead, legs, and tail with the #4 bright and Light Brown value. Wipe the brush and chisel-blend.

2. Thin Light Brown value and overlay the fur with liner strokes. Reload the brush often. As you stroke over the fur, let the brush run out of paint to help create variations in the values. You may overstroke the larger areas with the grainer to soften.

Fur, Step 4 – Detail:

1. Use the liner and Light Brown value to place final fluffs and highlights.
2. Use the liner and Titanium White to stroke the brightest highlights.

Tail:

1. Basecoat the tail with the Medium Brown value, using #4 bright brush.
2. Using choppy strokes with the Dark Brown value, place the darkest shading under the base of the tail. Apply some shading to the inner curve of the tail. Wipe the brush and chisel-blend.
3. Highlight with the Light Brown value. Wipe the brush and chisel-blend.
4. Highlight further with the liner and the Light Brown value.
5. Overlay the fur with many strokes of Light Brown value, using the grainer. Reload the brush often. As you stroke over the fur, let the brush run out of paint to help create variations in the values.
6. Apply the lightest highlight strokes with the liner and the Highlight Brown value.

Toes:

1. Basecoat the toes with the liner and the Medium Brown value.
2. Shade the toes with the Dark Brown value. Gently stipple-blend.
3. Highlight with the Light Brown value. Stipple-blend to soften.
4. Apply the lightest highlights with the Light Brown value.

Final Touches:

1. Use the liner and Dark Brown value to stipple the deepest shadows inside the ear. Wipe the brush and stipple-blend.
2. Use the liner and slightly thinned Burnt Sienna to stipple dots on the muzzle.
3. Use the liner and slightly thinned Titanium White to add highlights in the light brown area under the eye.

PAINT THE TABLE

Table:

Note: You may add a touch of Odorless Turpenoid to your brush to slightly thin the paint.

1. Use the #8 bright brush to basecoat the table with varying streaks of Burnt Sienna + Burnt Umber.
2. Shade under the table with Burnt Umber. Wipe the brush and streak the color from side to side.
3. Highlight the edge of the table with the Light Brown value. Let the table dry.

GLAZE THE FRUIT

The apple and cherries are much more vibrant and alive when a glaze is applied to intensify the shadows and highlights.

1. Allow the painting to dry completely.
2. Apply a thin layer of linseed oil to the apple and cherries, using the #8 bright.
3. Using the same brush, pick up a small amount of Alizarin Crimson and deepen the dark values. Wipe the brush.
4. Pick up a mix of Alizarin Crimson + Ivory Black and apply to the darkest areas. Wipe brush and blend into the linseed oil. Whisk the mop over the area to soften.
5. Use the #4 bright and Cadmium Yellow Light to highlight. Blend. Mop to soften.
6. Load the liner with a brush mix of Yellow Light + Titanium White. Tap a few glints onto fruit. Wipe brush and stipple-blend.

PAINT THE BACKGROUND

1. Mix equal parts Sap Green + Ultramarine Blue. Mix equal parts Sap Green + Prussian Blue.
2. Fill in the background with these two color mixes, using slip-slap strokes.
3. Near the table and edges, add Ivory Black to the mixture and continue to slip-slap.
4. Near the tail of the chipmunk, begin to slip-slap Titanium White into the mixture.
5. Wipe the brush and continue to soften the colors.
6. Finish with a mop brush to soften the brushstrokes.

FINISHING

1. Let the painting dry for at least ten days.
2. Apply five to ten coats of spray varnish, drying to the touch after each coat.

Chipmunk Painting Worksheet

1
Basecoat and apply the values.

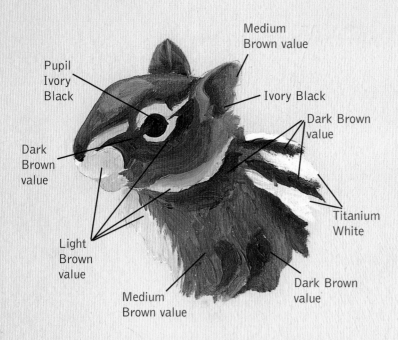

Pupil
Ivory
Black

Medium
Brown value

Ivory Black

Dark Brown
value

Dark
Brown
value

Light
Brown
value

Medium
Brown value

Dark Brown
value

Titanium
White

2
Blend with the chisel edge of the brush.

Shade with
Light Brown
value.

3
Strengthen shading and highlights.
Continue to blend.
Use the grainer in larger areas;
the liner in smaller areas.

Light Brown value

Bright
highlights
Titanium
White.

4
Detail with the liner.

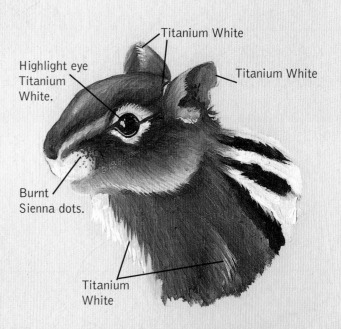

Titanium White

Highlight eye
Titanium
White.

Titanium White

Burnt
Sienna dots.

Titanium
White

Apple Painting Worksheet

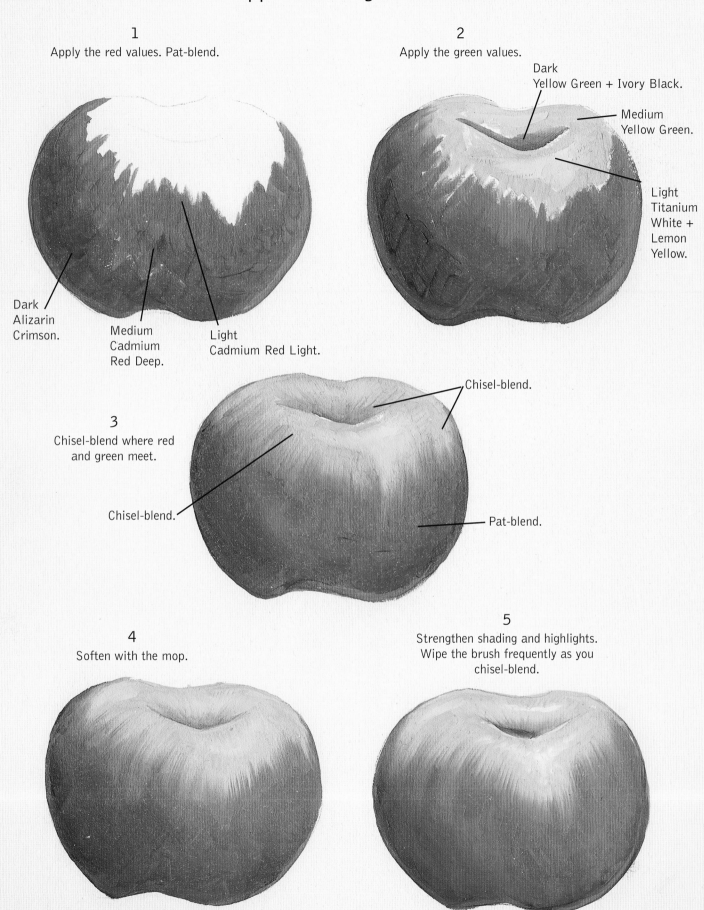

1
Apply the red values. Pat-blend.

Dark
Alizarin
Crimson.

Medium
Cadmium
Red Deep.

Light
Cadmium Red Light.

2
Apply the green values.

Dark
Yellow Green + Ivory Black.

Medium
Yellow Green.

Light
Titanium
White +
Lemon
Yellow.

3
Chisel-blend where red
and green meet.

Chisel-blend.

Chisel-blend.

Pat-blend.

4
Soften with the mop.

5
Strengthen shading and highlights.
Wipe the brush frequently as you
chisel-blend.

Squirrel & Berries

The forest provides for its small creatures; the juicy red berries are a feast for this little fellow. Create the soft fur by chisel-blending, then over-laying strokes with the grainer and the liner. The fine hairs at the outer edge of the tail show up well against the dark background.

SUPPLIES

Painting Surface

Canvas, 10" x 10"

Oil Palette

Alizarin Crimson

Burnt Sienna

Burnt Umber

Cadmium Red Deep

Cadmium Yellow Light

Ivory Black

Magenta

Raw Sienna

Sap Green

Titanium White

Ultramarine Blue

Yellow Ochre

Brushes

Bright – #4, #8

Flat Shader – #2, #10, #12

Grainer – ⅜"

Short Liner – 10/0

Wash – ¾"

Acrylic Background Colors

Burnt Umber

PREPARATION

Prepare the Surface:

Prepare the canvas, following the instructions in the "Surfaces" section of the "Supplies" chapter.

Basecoat the Surface:

1. Basecoat the canvas with Burnt Umber acrylic, using the wash brush. Let dry.
2. Apply as many coats as needed to achieve opaque coverage, drying after each coat.
3. Trace and transfer the design.

Color Mixes:

Premix the following oil color values with a palette knife:

- Highlight Brown: equal parts Yellow Ochre + Titanium White
- Light Brown: 1 part Titanium White + 1 part Medium Brown + a touch of Raw Sienna
- Medium Brown: 3 parts Burnt Umber + 1 part Titanium White + a touch of Burnt Sienna
- Dark Brown: equal parts Medium Brown + Burnt Umber

PAINT THE TREE BARK

1. Mix 1 part Dark Brown value + 1 part Titanium White + a touch of Ultramarine Blue. Basecoat the bark using the #8 bright. Wipe brush.
2. Use a mixture of Titanium White + a touch of Burnt Umber to highlight the outer edges of the nooks and crannies.
3. Wipe the brush. Add Ivory Black to shade each section.
4. With the liner and thinned Ivory Black, make squiggles and cracks in the bark. Make sure to go through some of the highlighted sections as well.
5. Add brighter highlights with the liner and Titanium White.
6. Add squiggly moss with the liner and thinned Sap Green.
7. Highlight the moss with a mixture of equal parts Sap Green + Cadmium Yellow Light + Titanium White.

PAINT THE SQUIRREL

See the Squirrel Painting Worksheet.

Eyes:

1. Paint the ring around the eye with the liner and the Light Brown value.
2. Basecoat the pupils with the liner and Ivory Black.

Continued on page 110

Continued from page 108

3. Use the liner and Titanium White to add little dots on the eye ring to highlight.

4. Highlight the pupil with a stroke of Titanium White on the lower left arc of the eye and two dots in the upper right, as shown on the Painting Worksheet.

Ears:

1. Basecoat the left inner ear with the liner and the Dark Brown value.

2. Basecoat the left outer ear with the liner and the Medium Brown value.

3. Mix a little Pink with equal parts Magenta + Titanium White. Referring to the Painting Worksheet, basecoat the right inner ear with Burnt Umber, Medium Brown value, and Pink mix. Gently pat-blend to connect and soften the values.

4. Basecoat the right outer ear with the Medium Brown value. Wipe the brush and pat-blend.

5. Highlight both outer ear edges with the liner and the Light Brown value. Wipe the brush and pat-blend.

6. Add the thin line on the outer ear and the tiny highlight strokes on the pink part of the inner ear with the liner and Titanium White.

Fur, Step 1 – Basecoat:

Use the chisel edge of the bright brush to apply the values.

1. Basecoat the light area on the nose, cheeks, chest/belly, and forehead with the Light Brown value.

2. Basecoat the rest of the fur with the Medium Brown value.

3. Apply Burnt Umber behind the cheek, around the light area near the eye, above and below the arm, under the belly, and in the darkest area of the tail next to the body.

4. Referring to the Painting Worksheet, basecoat the rest of the tail with the Medium Brown, the Dark Brown, and the Light Brown values, using the chisel edge of the brush.

Fur, Step 2 – Blend:

1. Blend with the chisel edge of the #4 bright brush, following the growth direction. Wipe the brush as needed. Remember that the fur strokes are shorter near the nose and around the eye and lengthen as you move away from the face.

2. Referring to the photo, continue to shade, highlight, and blend the fur on the body.

Fur, Step 3 – Overstroke:

1. Intensify the shading and highlighting using the grainer in large areas and the liner in small areas.

2. Thin Light Brown value and overlay the fur with liner strokes. Reload the brush often. As you stroke over the basecoat of the fur, let the brush run out of paint to help create variations in the values.

Fur, Step 4 – Detail:

Thin a mixture of Titanium White + a touch of Raw Sienna, and use the liner to add detail strokes and fur highlights. In a few areas, use Titanium White.

Forepaws & Toes:

1. Basecoat with the liner and the Medium Brown value.

2. With the liner and thinned Ivory Black, draw the separations between the digits.

3. Highlight with the liner and the Light Brown value. Stipple-blend to soften.

4. Apply the lightest highlights with the Highlight Brown value.

PAINT THE BERRIES

Branches:

1. Basecoat with the liner and thinned Burnt Sienna.

2. Highlight with the liner and streaks of Titanium White.

Berries:

1. Basecoat the berries with the liner and thinned Cadmium Red Deep.

2. Shade with Alizarin Crimson. The darkest shading will be opposite the highlights.

3. Thin a mixture of Alizarin Crimson + a touch of Ivory Black. Use the liner to draw a line to separate where one berry overlaps another.

4. With the liner and thinned Titanium White, add one or two highlights on the front of each berry.

PAINT THE BACKGROUND FOLIAGE

1. Using the #8 bright brush, slip-slap a background basecoat of Sap Green + Ivory Black.

Continued on page 112

Squirrel & Berries Painting Worksheet

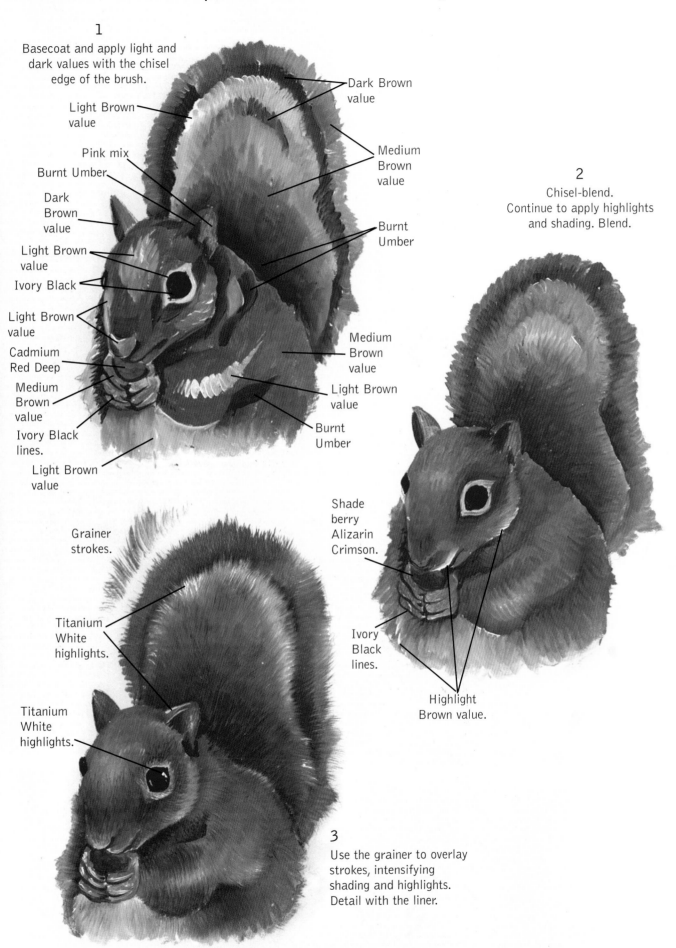

1
Basecoat and apply light and dark values with the chisel edge of the brush.

Dark Brown value

Light Brown value

Pink mix

Burnt Umber

Dark Brown value

Light Brown value

Ivory Black

Light Brown value

Cadmium Red Deep

Medium Brown value

Ivory Black lines.

Light Brown value

Medium Brown value

Burnt Umber

Medium Brown value

Light Brown value

Burnt Umber

2
Chisel-blend.
Continue to apply highlights and shading. Blend.

Shade berry Alizarin Crimson.

Ivory Black lines.

Highlight Brown value.

Grainer strokes.

Titanium White highlights.

Titanium White highlights.

3
Use the grainer to overlay strokes, intensifying shading and highlights. Detail with the liner.

Continued from page 110

2. Continue to layer strokes, varying the amount of each color, with more Sap Green toward the top.

3. Pick up Cadmium Yellow Light on the corner of the brush, and tap or stipple it into the upper background to suggest foliage.

FINISHING

1. Using the liner brush, tip the fur on the tail with Titanium White, blending the tail into the background.

2. Let the painting dry for at least ten days.

3. Apply five to ten coats of spray varnish, drying to the touch after each coat.

Pattern for Squirrel & Berries

The White Tiger

SUPPLIES

Painting Surface
Plaque with 9" round center panel

Oil Palette
Alizarin Crimson

Burnt Sienna

Burnt Umber

Cadmium Yellow Pale (Hue)

Cobalt Blue

French Ultramarine

Ivory Black

Raw Sienna

Titanium White

Brushes
Bright – #4, #8

Flat Shader – #0, #2, #10, #12

Grainer – ⅜"

Mop – ½"

Short Liner – 10/0

Wash – ¾"

Acrylic Background Colors
Mars Black

Titanium White

Other Supplies
Black Variegated Gold Leaf

Gold Leafing Basecoat, Size (Adhesive), and Shellac (Sealer)

Linseed Oil

The white tiger is one of my favorite creatures to paint. Its creamy white fur with chocolate brown stripes contrast dramatically with its clear blue eyes and pink nose. Tigers are a protected species worldwide and not often found in the wild, which is why capturing a glimpse in paint is so exciting!

PREPARATION

Prepare the Surface:
Prepare the plaque, following the instructions in the "Surfaces" section of the "Supplies" chapter.

Basecoat the Surface:
1. Basecoat the surface with Mars Black acrylic, using the wash brush. Let dry. Apply as many coats as needed to achieve opaque coverage, drying after each coat.
2. Trace and transfer the outline of the tiger.
3. Basecoat the tiger with an equal mix of acrylic Mars Black and Titanium White. Use the grainer to pull out the fur ends.

Apply the Gold Leaf:
Refer to the "Metal Leafing" instructions in the "General Information & Techniques" section.
1. Apply the black variegated gold leaf to the decorative rim of the plaque, following the manufacturer's instructions.
2. Shellac only the gold leafing. Let dry.

Color Mixes:
Premix the following oil color values with a palette knife:
- Medium Gray: Titanium White + a touch of Burnt Umber + a touch of Ivory Black
- Light Gray: equal parts Medium Gray + Titanium White
- Dark Gray: equal parts Medium Gray + Ivory Black

PAINT THE TIGER

Note: To maintain the sharp contrast of the fur values, wipe the brush on a paper towel between applying the different values.

Eyes:
See the White Tiger Eye & Fur Painting Worksheet.
1. Using the liner and Ivory Black, paint the black rim around the eye.
2. Mix 1 part Cobalt Blue + 1 part French Ultramarine + a touch of Titanium White. Basecoat the irises.
3. Use the liner to apply French Ultramarine at the tops of the eyes. Wipe the brush and gently tap to blend.

Continued on page 116

Continued from page 114

4. Using the liner and Titanium White, add a thin line to the lower edge of each iris. Wipe the liner. Using multiple liner strokes, pull the white toward the center of the pupil.

5. Basecoat the pupils with the liner and thinned Ivory Black.

6. Use the liner to apply a Titanium White highlight stroke to each eye, positioning it half on the iris and half on the pupil. Add a Titanium White highlight dot to the lower right side of each pupil. Refer to the Painting Worksheet for placement.

Nose:
See the White Tiger Nose Painting Worksheet.

1. Mix equal parts Ivory Black + Burnt Umber. Use the liner to basecoat the nostrils and the area between the nose and the mouth.

2. Mix 1 part Burnt Sienna + 1 part Titanium White + a touch of Alizarin Crimson. Use the #4 bright brush to basecoat the nose.

3. Wipe the brush. Pick up Titanium White, apply sparingly to the top of the nose, and pat-blend.

4. Wipe the brush. Shade the underside of the nose with Burnt Sienna. Wipe the brush and pat-blend.

5. Stipple Burnt Sienna with the liner inside the triangular black opening under the nose. Wipe the brush and pat-blend.

6. Add bright highlights on the nose and nostrils with the liner and broken lines of Titanium White.

7. Add a few Titanium White marks to highlight the lower lip.

Ears:

1. Use the chisel edge of the #4 bright brush and the Dark Gray value to basecoat the inner ears, following the fur growth direction.

2. Basecoat the outer rims with the Light Gray value. Pat-blend the two values to soften.

3. Using the grainer and Titanium White, highlight the outer rims, pulling tufts of fur onto the background.

4. Wipe the grainer. Pull the Dark Gray value of the inner ear over the tops of the rims of the ears.

5. Wipe the grainer. Accent the fringe just below the ear with Titanium White + a touch of French Ultramarine. Pull fur over the inner ear.

Fur Around the Eyes:
See the White Tiger Eye & Fur Painting Worksheet.

1. Use the chisel edge of the #2 flat brush for the tiny areas around the eye. Apply Titanium White to the light areas and Ivory Black to the dark areas around the eyes. Wipe the brush. Where the white and black meet under the eye, place the chisel edge of the brush on both colors, and softly wiggle from side to side to connect the two areas.

2. Use the liner and thinned Ivory Black to overlap the white area with eyelashes.

3. Use the liner to add small dots of Titanium White within the dark rim of each eye.

Muzzle:
See the White Tiger Nose Painting Worksheet.

1. Use short strokes with the grainer and the Dark Gray value to basecoat the dark stripes and markings on the muzzle.

2. Wipe the brush. Overlay the dark stripes with a slightly lighter value of gray to soften them.

3. Use the grainer and the Light Gray value to paint the light areas on the muzzle.

4. Wipe the brush. Overlay the light areas near the edge of each cheek with the Medium Gray value.

5. Use the liner to highlight near the nose with stippled or patted on Titanium White + a touch of Raw Sienna.

6. Use the liner with thinned Ivory Black to add a few darker lines and dots to the muzzle. Let dry.

Basecoat the Stripes:
Note: To maintain the sharp contrast of the black-and-white values, blend by placing the chisel edge of the brush where the values meet and wiggling the brush slightly from side to side. Wipe the brush frequently.

1. Begin applying the white fur on the outer fringe with the Dark Gray value. Lighten the values as you stroke toward the nose and eye area, changing to Medium Gray value, then Light Gray value. As you continue toward the nose area, shorten the fur strokes.

2. Basecoat the black stripes with equal parts Ivory Black + Burnt Umber, using the chisel edge of the brush and following the fur growth direction. Wipe the brush and blend with the chisel edge.

3. Basecoat above the nose with short strokes of the Medium Gray value.

Highlight & Shade the Stripes:

1. Use the grainer to add an overlay of Titanium White highlight strokes to all light fur areas. Allow the highlight strokes to overlap the black stripes. Wipe the brush frequently.

2. Highlight the center of the snout with Titanium White. Use extremely short strokes to create the fur. Wipe the brush frequently.

3. Use the grainer to shade above the nose and in the front corner of the eyes with the Dark Gray value. Use a sparse amount of paint. Wipe the brush and soften into the fur, always following the growth direction. You will need to wipe the brush every stroke or two to keep the color pure.

Detail the Fur:

1. Highlight under the eyes with the liner and thinned Titanium White.

2. Use the liner with Titanium White to brighten some highlights. Further brighten a few select areas with touches of Titanium White. Refer to the photograph for placement.

Chin:

See the White Tiger Nose Painting Worksheet.

1. Use the chisel edge of the #4 bright brush to basecoat the chin with the Medium Gray value, following the fur growth direction.

2. Use the grainer with the Dark Gray value to shade near the mouth. Allow the brush to run out of paint as you stroke from the mouth outward.

3. Use the liner and thinned Dark Gray value to dot a few lines on the highlighted portion of the muzzle.

4. With the liner and Burnt Sienna, stipple some tiny dots in a curve under the lower lip.

5. Add a few final highlights with the liner and thinned Titanium White.

PAINT THE BACKGROUND & LEAVES

Background:

Paint this as close to the tiger as possible.

1. Basecoat the background with the #8 bright brush and Ivory Black. Slip-slap the color, moving the brush in different directions.

2. Mix equal parts French Ultramarine + Titanium White. Pick up Cadmium Yellow Pale or the blue mix, and work into the black basecoat with slip-slap strokes. It doesn't matter if the final tint is more green or more blue, but the background should be almost black.

Leaves:

1. Mix a medium green value with 5 parts Cadmium Yellow Pale + 1 part Ivory Black + a touch of Titanium White. Basecoat the leaves.

2. Apply Ivory Black shading near the center vein. Chisel-blend out into the medium green value. Wipe the brush frequently so as not to pick up too much paint.

3. Highlight the leaf edges with a mixture of equal parts Cadmium Yellow Pale + Titanium White. Wipe the brush and chisel-blend back toward the vein line.

4. Accent some areas of the leaves with a mixture of equal parts French Ultramarine + Titanium White.

5. Accent other leaf areas with Burnt Sienna.

ACCENTS & FINAL TOUCHES

1. Accent the very outer fringe with an overlay of a mix of equal parts Titanium White + French Ultramarine. Apply this cool accent sparingly with the grainer and do not completely cover the layers beneath.

2. To highlight the forehead, use the liner to overlay strokes of thinned Light Gray value. Do not completely cover the layers beneath.

3. Pull lines and tufts from the chin and muzzle with thinned Titanium White, using the grainer and the liner.

4. Allow the painting to dry. Use the liner to add fine detail lines, especially around the eyes, nose, and mouth.

5. Whiskers are optional. If desired, add them with the liner and Titanium White after the tiger is dry.

GLAZING

If the fur appears too coarse in some areas, soften the look by glazing with colors from the palette. Intensify shadows or highlights. An example would be the fur above the nose. Moisten the area and intensify the highlight by working Titanium White into the brush and applying to the highlight area of the fur. Wipe the brush and blend the color into the glaze.

1. Allow the painting to dry completely.

2. Apply a thin layer of linseed oil to the area.

3. Using the same brush, pick up a small amount of the shading or highlight color from your palette and work it into the bristles. Apply the transparent color to the moistened area, wipe the brush, and blend the color into the area.

4. If desired, mop to soften.

FINISHING

1. Let the painting dry for at least ten days.

2. Apply five to ten coats of spray varnish, drying to the touch after each coat.

The White Tiger Eye & Fur Painting Worksheet

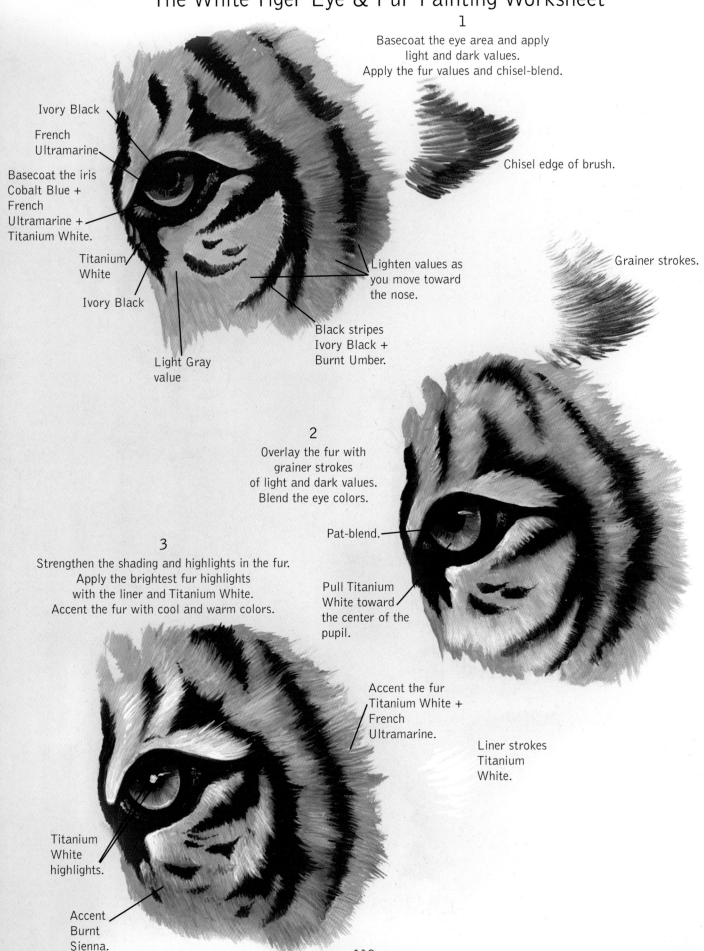

1
Basecoat the eye area and apply
light and dark values.
Apply the fur values and chisel-blend.

Chisel edge of brush.

Ivory Black

French
Ultramarine

Basecoat the iris
Cobalt Blue +
French
Ultramarine +
Titanium White.

Titanium
White

Ivory Black

Light Gray
value

Lighten values as
you move toward
the nose.

Black stripes
Ivory Black +
Burnt Umber.

Grainer strokes.

2
Overlay the fur with
grainer strokes
of light and dark values.
Blend the eye colors.

Pat-blend.

3
Strengthen the shading and highlights in the fur.
Apply the brightest fur highlights
with the liner and Titanium White.
Accent the fur with cool and warm colors.

Pull Titanium
White toward
the center of the
pupil.

Accent the fur
Titanium White +
French
Ultramarine.

Liner strokes
Titanium
White.

Titanium
White
highlights.

Accent
Burnt
Sienna.

118

The White Tiger Nose Painting Worksheet

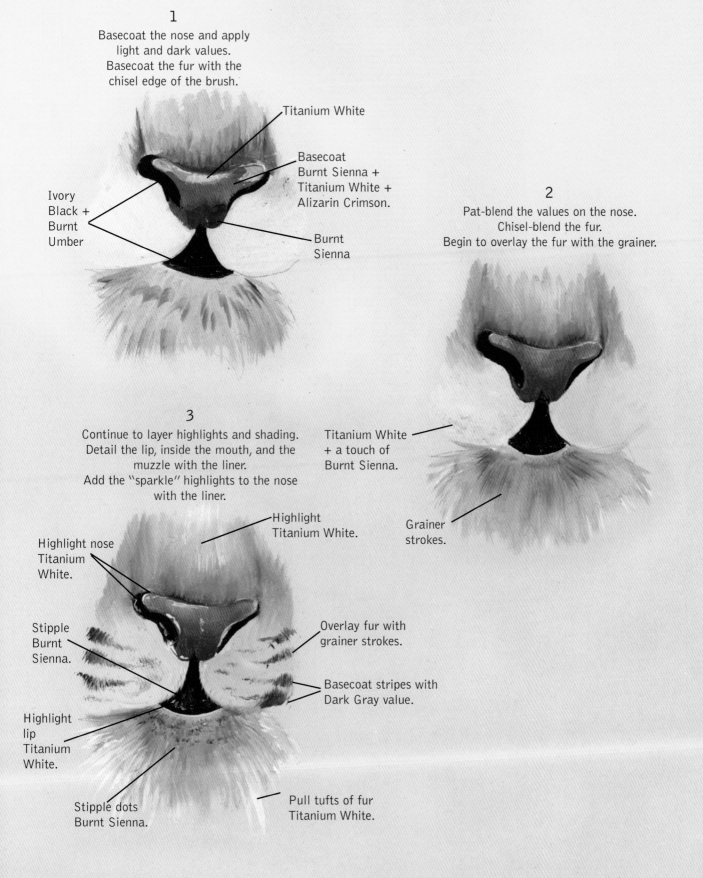

1
Basecoat the nose and apply light and dark values. Basecoat the fur with the chisel edge of the brush.

Titanium White

Basecoat
Burnt Sienna +
Titanium White +
Alizarin Crimson.

Ivory Black + Burnt Umber

Burnt Sienna

2
Pat-blend the values on the nose. Chisel-blend the fur. Begin to overlay the fur with the grainer.

Titanium White + a touch of Burnt Sienna.

Grainer strokes.

3
Continue to layer highlights and shading. Detail the lip, inside the mouth, and the muzzle with the liner. Add the "sparkle" highlights to the nose with the liner.

Highlight Titanium White.

Highlight nose Titanium White.

Stipple Burnt Sienna.

Highlight lip Titanium White.

Overlay fur with grainer strokes.

Basecoat stripes with Dark Gray value.

Stipple dots Burnt Sienna.

Pull tufts of fur Titanium White.

Pattern for The White Tiger

Pattern for the Bengal Tiger – Night Gaze

Instructions begin on page 122.

Bengal Tiger–Night Gaze

The Bengal tiger is one of nature's fiercest, most territorial creatures. Its combination of power, masterful hunting ability, and watchful stance enthralls people all over the world. Sadly, due to the beauty of its fur and the decline of its natural habitat, its population has rapidly decreased and the Bengal tiger is now an endangered species. I encourage you to support the world's efforts in maintaining their precious existence.

SUPPLIES

Painting Surface
Basket with Wooden Lid

Oil Palette
Alizarin Crimson
Burnt Sienna
Burnt Umber
Cadmium Yellow Pale (Hue)
Cobalt Blue
French Ultramarine
Ivory Black
Raw Sienna
Sap Green
Titanium White
Venetian Red
Yellow Ochre

Brushes
Bright – #4, #8
Flat Shader – #2, #10, #12
Grainer – ⅜"
Mop – ½"
Short Liner – 10/0
Wash – ¾"

Acrylic Background Colors
Brilliant Ultramarine

Other Supplies
Black Variegated Gold Leaf
Gold Leafing Basecoat, Size
   (Adhesive), and Shellac (Sealer)

PREPARATION

Prepare the Surface:
Prepare the surface, following the instructions in the "Surfaces" section of the "Supplies" chapter.

Basecoat the Surface:
1. Basecoat the surface with Brilliant Ultramarine acrylic, using the wash brush. Let dry.
2. Apply as many coats as needed to achieve opaque coverage, drying after each coat.
3. Trace and transfer the design.

Apply the Gold Leaf:
Refer to the "Metal Leafing" instructions in the "General Information & Techniques" section.
1. Apply the black variegated gold leaf to the decorative rim of the plaque, following the manufacturer's instructions.
2. Shellac only the gold leafing. Let dry.

Color Mixes:
Premix the following oil color values with a palette knife:
• Highlight: equal parts Yellow Ochre + Titanium White
• Light Brown: 2 parts Yellow Ochre + 1 part Medium Brown
• Medium Brown: equal parts Raw Sienna + Burnt Sienna
• Dark Brown: Burnt Sienna
• Low Dark Brown: equal parts Burnt Sienna + Burnt Umber

PAINT THE TIGER

Eye:
See the Bengal Tiger Face Details Painting Worksheet.
1. Basecoat the iris with the liner and Cobalt Blue.
2. Apply French Ultramarine near the back of the eye with the liner. Wipe the brush and gently tap to blend.
3. Using the liner, add a thin line of Titanium White to the lower right edge of the eye. Wipe the liner. Using multiple liner strokes, pull the highlight toward the center of the pupil.
4. Basecoat the pupil with the liner and thinned Ivory Black.
5. Using the liner, apply a Titanium White highlight positioned half on the iris and half on the pupil. Add Titanium White highlights to the left corner and lower right edge of the eye, as shown on the Painting Worksheet.

Nose:

See the Bengal Tiger Face Details Painting Worksheet.

1. Mix equal parts Ivory Black + Burnt Umber. Use the liner to basecoat the nostrils and the area between the nose and the mouth.

2. Mix 1 part Burnt Sienna + 1 part Titanium White + a touch of Alizarin Crimson. Use the #4 bright brush to basecoat the nose.

3. Wipe the brush. Pick up Titanium White, apply sparingly to the nostrils and tip of the nose, and pat-blend.

4. Wipe the brush. Shade the underside of the nose with the Ivory Black + Burnt Umber mixture. Wipe the brush and pat-blend.

5. Add bright highlights on the nose and nostrils with the liner and broken lines of Titanium White. Avoid placing highlights in a solid line.

Ears:

1. Working out toward the outer rim of the ear, basecoat the inner ear with the Low Dark Brown value, Dark Brown value (Burnt Sienna), and then the Medium Brown value. Use the chisel edge of the #4 bright brush and roughly chop the values together, following the fur growth direction.

Continued on page next page

Continued from page 123

2. Wipe the brush. Apply the Light Brown value to define the rim of the ear. On the right side of the foreground ear, connect the outer rim to the inner ear using the chisel edge of the brush.

3. Use the liner and the Highlight value to highlight the outer rim, pulling tufts of fur onto the background.

4. Basecoat the outer ears with the #4 bright brush and the Dark Brown value (Burnt Sienna).

5. Shade near the rim of the ear with the Low Dark Brown value. Wipe the brush and gently chisel-blend.

Note: To maintain the sharp contrast of the black and brown values, blend by placing the chisel edge of the brush where the values meet and wiggling the brush slightly from side to side. Wipe the brush frequently.

Fur Around the Eye:

See the Bengal Tiger Face Details Painting Worksheet.

1. Use the liner with slightly thinned Low Dark Brown value to apply the dark area around the eye.

2. Highlight under the eye with the liner and thinned Titanium White.

3. Pick up Burnt Sienna and tap a highlight near the front of the eye.

4. Wipe the brush. Pick up Yellow Ochre, and add further highlight strokes.

5. Using the chisel edge of a small bright brush, chisel-blend the fur values. Wipe the brush frequently.

6. Using the grainer, overlay the fur with the Highlight value. Allow the strokes to overlap the darker fur values. Reload the brush frequently.

7. Using the liner, add tiny strokes of Titanium White for sparkling highlights.

Fringe & Fur:

1. Use the chisel edge of a bright brush with the Low Dark Brown value mix to basecoat the black stripes, following the fur growth direction.

2. Begin to basecoat above the nose with the Medium Brown value. Carry this value from above the nose, around the eye, and under the chin.

3. Shade above the nose and in the front corner of the eye with the Low Dark Brown value. Wipe the brush and chisel-blend, following the fur growth direction.

4. Highlight the center of the snout with the Light Brown value. Wipe the brush and chisel-blend.

5. Basecoat the remainder of the fur with the Light Brown value.

6. Overlap the Light Brown value over the dark stripes, using the chisel edge of the brush. Wipe the brush often, as you continue to pick up paint.

Highlight & Shade the Stripes:

Use the grainer to add an overlay of the Highlight value to all Light Brown fur areas. Allow the Highlight value to overlay the black stripes. Reload the brush frequently because it will pick up color while you are painting.

Detail the Fur:

1. Highlight under the eye with the liner and thinned Titanium White.

2. Use the liner with the Highlight value to brighten the fur in some highlighted areas.

3. Further brighten a few select areas with touches of Titanium White. Refer to the photograph for placement.

Muzzle:

See the Bengal Tiger Face Details Painting Worksheet.

1. Basecoat the muzzle near the nose and mouth with the #4 bright brush and the Light Brown value.

2. Gradually pick up increasing amounts of the Medium Brown value as you basecoat where the black markings will be applied.

3. Roughly highlight the muzzle near the nose and mouth with thinned Highlight value. Wipe the brush and chisel-blend.

4. Use the liner with thinned Low Dark Brown value to apply the dark markings.

5. Use the liner and thinned Low Dark Brown value to add a few dots on the highlighted portion of the muzzle.

Chin:

1. Use the chisel edge of the #4 bright brush to basecoat the chin with the Medium Brown value, following the fur growth direction.

2. Use the grainer and Burnt Sienna (the Dark Brown value) to shade near the mouth. Allow the brush to run out of paint as you stroke from the mouth outward.

3. Add a few final highlights with the liner and thinned Titanium White.

PAINT THE BACKGROUND

1. Mix equal parts Cobalt Blue + French Ultramarine. Slip-slap the color, moving the brush in different directions.

2. Pick up Titanium White and slip-slap highlights into various areas. Wipe the brush and soften into the background.

3. Apply some Sap Green to the lower right corner.

4. Using the liner and thinned Yellow Ochre, pull strokes of grass from the lower right. Allow the brush to run out of paint in order to create variations in the grass color.

Continued on page 126

Bengal Tiger Face Details Painting Worksheet

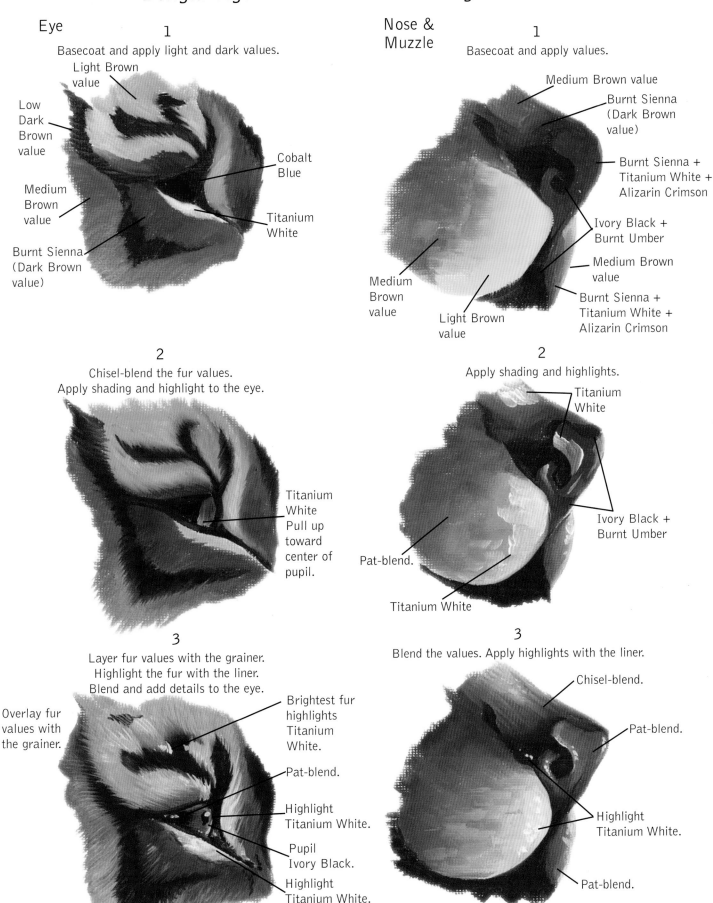

Eye

1
Basecoat and apply light and dark values.

Light Brown value

Low Dark Brown value

Medium Brown value

Burnt Sienna (Dark Brown value)

Cobalt Blue

Titanium White

2
Chisel-blend the fur values.
Apply shading and highlight to the eye.

Titanium White
Pull up toward center of pupil.

3
Layer fur values with the grainer.
Highlight the fur with the liner.
Blend and add details to the eye.

Overlay fur values with the grainer.

Brightest fur highlights Titanium White.

Pat-blend.

Highlight Titanium White.

Pupil Ivory Black.

Highlight Titanium White.

Nose & Muzzle

1
Basecoat and apply values.

Medium Brown value

Burnt Sienna (Dark Brown value)

Burnt Sienna + Titanium White + Alizarin Crimson

Ivory Black + Burnt Umber

Medium Brown value

Burnt Sienna + Titanium White + Alizarin Crimson

Medium Brown value

Light Brown value

2
Apply shading and highlights.

Titanium White

Ivory Black + Burnt Umber

Pat-blend.

Titanium White

3
Blend the values. Apply highlights with the liner.

Chisel-blend.

Pat-blend.

Highlight Titanium White.

Pat-blend.

125

Continued from page 124

5. Add a touch of thinned Cadmium Yellow Pale to high-light a few blades of grass.
6. Mop to soften and blend the colors.

FINAL TOUCHES

1. Allow the painting to dry. Use the liner to add fine detail lines, especially around the eyes, nose, and mouth.
2. Whiskers are optional. If desired, add them with the liner and Titanium White after the tiger is dry.

GLAZING

If the fur appears too coarse in some areas, soften the look by glazing with colors from the palette. Intensify shadows or highlights.

1. Allow the painting to dry completely.
2. Apply a thin layer of linseed oil to the area.
3. Using the same brush, pick up a small amount of the shading or highlight color from your palette and work it into the bristles. Apply the transparent color to the moistened area, wipe the brush, and blend the color into the area.
4. If desired, glaze Venetian Red above the nose and any-where you would like a warmer value on the tiger.
5. If desired, mop to soften.

FINISHING

1. Let the painting dry for at least ten days.
2. Apply five to ten coats of spray varnish, drying to the touch after each coat.

Metric Conversion Chart

Inches to Millimeters and Centimeters

Inches	MM	CM	Inches	MM	CM
1/8	3	.3	2	51	5.1
1/4	6	.6	3	76	7.6
3/8	10	1.0	4	102	10.2
1/2	13	1.3	5	127	12.7
5/8	16	1.6	6	152	15.2
3/4	19	1.9	7	178	17.8
7/8	22	2.2	8	203	20.3
1	25	2.5	9	229	22.9
1-1/4	32	3.2	10	254	25.4
1-1/2	38	3.8	11	279	27.9
1-3/4	44	4.4	12	305	30.5

Yards to Meters

Yards	Meters	Yards	Meters
1/8	.11	3	2.74
1/4	.23	4	3.66
3/8	.34	5	4.57
1/2	.46	6	5.49
5/8	.57	7	6.40
3/4	.69	8	7.32
7/8	.80	9	8.23
1	.91	10	9.14
2	1.83		

Index

A
Acrylics 14, 30, 32, 36, 40, 44, 50, 58, 62, 68, 74, 82, 86, 94, 102, 108, 114, 122
  artists' tube 14
  bottled artists' pigments 14
  premixed craft 14
Angels 62
Animals, painting 27
Apple 107

B
Baby Bunny & Magnolias 86
Baby Ducks 57, 58, 61
Baby oil 16
Background
  eggshell finish 19
  parchment 20
  slip-slap 20
Basecoating 23
Basin, water 15
Basket 122
Bengal Tiger—Night Gaze 122
Berries 108
Bird, painting 26
Blending 24
Blending diagram
  baby ducks 81
  chickadee 55

Blue Jay 82, 84, 85
Bowl 32, 40
Brush(es) 10, 15
  bright(s) 10, 30, 32, 36, 40, 44, 50, 58, 62, 68, 74, 82, 86, 94, 102, 108, 114, 122
  care 11, 15
  flat shader 10, 36, 40, 44, 50, 58, 62, 68, 74, 82, 86, 94, 102, 108, 114, 122
  grainer 11, 25, 58, 82, 86, 94, 102, 108, 114, 122
  liner 10, 30, 32, 36, 40, 44, 50, 58, 62, 68, 74, 82, 86, 94, 102, 108, 114, 122
  loading 23
  mixing 23
  mop 11, 62, 102, 114, 122
  wash 10, 30, 32, 36, 40, 44, 50, 58, 62, 68, 74, 82, 86, 94, 102, 108, 114, 122
Bunny 86, 90
Butterfly(ies) 27, 30, 32, 34, 36, 38, 40, 43, 44, 47, 52

C
Canvas 17, 36, 50, 58, 94, 102, 108
Canvas paper 30
Cherry(ies) 50, 52

Chickadee 50, 53
Chickadee & Cherries 50
Chipmunk & Fruit 102
Chisel-blending 24, 27
Cloth, soft 16, 68
Color conversion chart 14
Columbine 71
Conure 74, 77

D
Decoupage 21
Decoupage medium 36
Doe in the Forest 94
Dry-wipe 23
Ducks 57, 58, 61

E
Eggshell finish 19
Eraser 16
Exotic Butterfly Bowl 32
Exotic Duo 74

F
Finishing 23
Floating 23
Foam roller 16, 50, 76, 82, 86
Forest 94
Fruit 102

Continued on next page

G
General techniques 18
Glazing 23
Gold leaf(ing) 21
    pen 17, 32, 44
    products 17, 32, 114, 122
    variegated 32, 114, 122
Grainer, using 25
Guardian Angels Plaque 62

H
Hardboard 17
Hummingbird 65, 62, 68, 70

I
Information, general 18
Ink 17, 36
Introduction 8

J
Jar 16
Journal 68

L
Leaves, painting 28
Lily 66
Linseed oil 12

M
Macaw 74, 77, 78
Magnolias 86, 91
Masonite 17
    panel(s) 44, 74, 82
Medium(s) 14
    acrylic 14
    blending gel 14, 68
    floating 14
    glazing 14
    texture 17, 30, 32, 44, 62
Metal 17

O
Orchids 44, 47
Overlay 23
Overstroke 23

P
Painter's tape 16, 36
Painting terms 23
Painting
    animals 26
    birds 25
    butterflies 26
    leaves 27
    supplies 10
Paints
    acrylic 14, 30, 32, 36, 40, 44, 50,
        58, 62, 68, 74, 82, 86, 94, 102,
        108, 114, 122

oil 12, 30, 32, 36, 40, 44, 50, 58,
    62, 68, 74, 82, 86, 94, 102,
    108, 114, 122
Palette 15, 16
    knife 16
    oil 13
Paper bag 16
Paper towels 16
Papers, decorative with letters 36
Parchment background 20
Paste, metallic rub-on 62
Pat-blending 24, 27
Pattern
    baby bunny & magnolias 93
    baby ducks 57
    Bengal tiger 121
    blue jay 84
    bromeliad stencil 35
    butterfly 30, 32, 39
    chickadee & cherries 56
    chipmunk 101
    conure 81
    doe 100
    guardian angels plaque 67
    hummingbird & columbine 73
    macaw 81
    orchid 48
    pink orchids & butterfly 49
    squirrel 113
    vanessa 39
    white tiger 120
Peacock Butterfly Canvas 36
Pen 16
Penholder 40
Pencil 16
Pink Orchids & Butterfly 44
Plaque 62, 86, 114
Plate 44
Projects 29

R
Ruby-Throated Hummingbird
    Journal 68
Ruler 16

S
Sandpaper 16
Shading diagram
    baby ducks 81
    bunny 89
Simply Beautiful Butterfly 30
Slip-slap background 20
Sponge 36
Squirrel & Berries 108
Stencil
    flourishes and frills 44, 62
    leaf 32, 36
    scrollwork 30, 40

Stenciling 21
    textured 22
Stipple-blending 25
Stylus 16
Supplies
    additional 16
    painting 10
Surfaces 17

T
Techniques
    blending 24
    general 18
Template, circle 32
The White Tiger 114
Thinner 12
Tiger 114, 122
Tips, painting 25
Tools, general 16
Toothbrush 82, 86
Tracing paper 16
Transfer paper 16
Transferring the design 23

V
Vanessa 40
Varnish 17

W
Water 16
Wood 17
Worksheet
    apple 107
    baby ducks 61
    Bengal tiger 125
    blue jay 85
    bunny 90
    butterfly 30, 34, 38, 47, 55
    cherry 55
    chickadee 53
    chipmunk 106
    columbine 71
    doe 98, 99
    exotic duo 77
    grainer 28
    hummingbird 65, 70
    leaves 27
    lily 66
    macaw 78
    magnolia 91
    pink orchids 47
    squirrel 111
    Vanessa 43
    white tiger eye & fur 118
    white tiger nose 119

I absolutely love to create cool background effects
and add embellishments.
It adds professionalism to your work and creates interest
to the viewer. The trick with embellishments is to PLAY!
All you need are some leafing supplies, acrylic ink,
modeling paste and a little paint to create endless effects
on paper, glass, canvas and wood.

creates interest

A Message From Willow...

Art is an integral part of our personal and cultural health and expression. As we learn to paint and draw we build skills and combine knowledge, increasing confidence and creating a sense of accomplishment. When I began teaching over 12 years ago the greatest joy was in watching each individual grow and create. I have since watched many students become designers and instructors to fulfill personal and career aspirations.

Artists, designers and teachers use various tools to create. Great tools are the cornerstone of great work. The Artograph DesignMaster Projector is a tool that allows the designer to place design elements and resize objects with ease. An artist can combine photographs of the birds and wildlife they see around them, project the image directly on a canvas and sketch an outline of their very own choosing. Combine flowers with your favorite bird, or a butterfly with your favorite animal. Most importantly enjoy the process, relax and have fun!!!

With Love,
Willow Wolfe